Merry Xmas Boyd.
from Bill & Doris
XMAS 97

CELTIC
MYTHOLOGY

CELTIC MYTHOLOGY

SIMON GOODENOUGH

TIGER

This edition published in 1997 by
Tiger Books International PLC, Twickenham

This book was designed and produced by
Todtri Productions Limited P.O. Box 572, New York,
NY 10116-0572 FAX: (212) 279-1241

Printed and bound in Singapore

ISBN 1-85501-931-0

Contents

Introduction

Celtic myths and legends introduce an extraordinary world of imagination, a world that gains strength and credibility because it stems from the real lives of the ancient Celts. Like all myths, the tales are largely an attempt to explain the universe, to come to terms with life and death and the changing seasons, on which, as a people who lived off the land, the Celts so greatly depended. Their legends also portray the human spirit, the ambitions and desires, aspirations and fears, of fellow humans two thousand years ago. Between the human world and the "Otherworld," the gods and heroes of Celtic mythology move gracefully, with an ease that lends dignity and richness to the beliefs and everyday lives of some our ancestors and to our own heritage.

Above: Pagan Theme, *a 1985 painting by Gordon Wain. Celtic traditions survive in art today, while their pagan themes predate Christianity. Much of the creative tension in Celtic myth is between pagan and Christian themes, but the ram had a place in both traditions.*

Opposite: Stonehenge, *or the Giant's Ring, is the most famous of the megalithic sites and dates back to before 2000 B.C., when its bluestone pillars were transported from Wales. It stands on Salisbury Plain, in Wiltshire, England, and was a prominent place of worship for the Celtic Druids.*

The Celts did not live as a single organized nation and are difficult to pin down to one specific way of life or set of beliefs. They had no fixed pantheon of gods and often had different names for gods who had similar functions among different tribes. They were a loose collection of tribal people: imaginative, artistic, warlike, not uncivilized but uncluttered by civilization. This intriguing mix of attributes makes thier mythology especially fascinating.

Their stories are engaging and infectious: Our spirits are raised by their heroics, our hearts moved by their passions and tragedies, our senses sharpened by their dangers and conflicts, our curiosity aroused by their superb skills in storytelling. They can shock us, too, by the amorality of their actions, and by the disconcerting tension between loyalty and deceit. We are left with a powerful image of people who challenged life head-on in harsh times and triumphed.

The Celts lived in the centuries around the birth of Christ, but their tales lie at the heart of many medieval romances, and the imaginative themes within those tales steal a march on many themes in modern science fiction. Gods and heroes intermingle as readily as modern aliens and Earth people; time can be bent in almost any direction; shape-shifters use their supernatural skills to transform themselves and thus evade pursuit or disrupt an enemy.

We could not hope for a greater range of characters from any fictional or true-life saga in any age of history: the omnipotent, omniscient god; the sexuality and power of the fertility goddess; the haglike goddess of death; deities with triple identities, images with triple heads; the beautiful, alluring young maiden fit for heroes to win through the performance of magnificent deeds; the warrior kings, champions and protectors of their people, the mediators between tribe members and gods; the young challengers from outside the tribe, the heroes who risk all and dare anything to win glory; the loyal henchmen, the traitors, the wise teachers, the magicians, sorcerers, witches, banshees, gifted people, seers, and skilled artisans; the poets, bards, diviners, faithful fools, satirists, storytellers, and orators whom warriors invoke to sing their praises and argue their causes; good and evil, sacred and profane, young and old, men and women, friend, family, foe, and the fearsome forces of the dark.

Magical accoutrements—slings, spears, swords, silver branches, mystical music, and cauldrons of plenty—enable heroes and gods to become a match for any power on earth or beyond. Irreversible curses condemn warriors to fateful obligations and honorable deaths. Severed heads speak oracles. Giant wickerwork bonfires contain horrendous human sacrifices. Invincible but vulnerable heroes mix with magical swans and with swine that can be eaten, recover, and be eaten again. For the heroes, there are distant islands of the unknown, otherworlds, underworlds, sacred rivers, islands, and hills. For the tribesfolk, there are great festivals to challenge the grim cold of winter and welcome the new spring or celebrate the summer harvest.

Threaded through all of this, there is the solid reality of Celtic life: farming communities struggling to survive, relying on the strength of family ties to control their more discordant elements, seeking relief from uncertainty and danger, anxious for security and protection as well as advantage and glory. The Celts understood the vibrancy of life and the fatalism of death; they sought harmony with nature, aspired to artistic elegance, set the highest value on loyalty, and rewarded the brave with promises of a magical afterlife. We owe to them much of our inheritance.

In the short space of this book, it is possible to give only a glimpse of a very few of the characters and incidents from Celtic myth and legend and to provide a fleeting sketch of the Celtic way of life. Our hope is that these images, in words and pictures, will encourage readers to look further afield and discover more for themselves about these extraordinary people.

Above: A Roman statue of a chained captive Celt from Gaul, first century A.D., Provence. Much of what we know about the Celts comes down to us from firsthand observation by the invading Romans. But the Romans themselves may have distorted history to emphasize their own prowess and superiority. The strong physique of the Celts, however, seems to have been in no doubt.

Opposite: The Romans often zealously paraded their military victories through the lands they conquered. This sculpture of captive Gauls is part of a triumphal arch in Provence.

THE WORLD OF
CELTIC
MYTHOLOGY

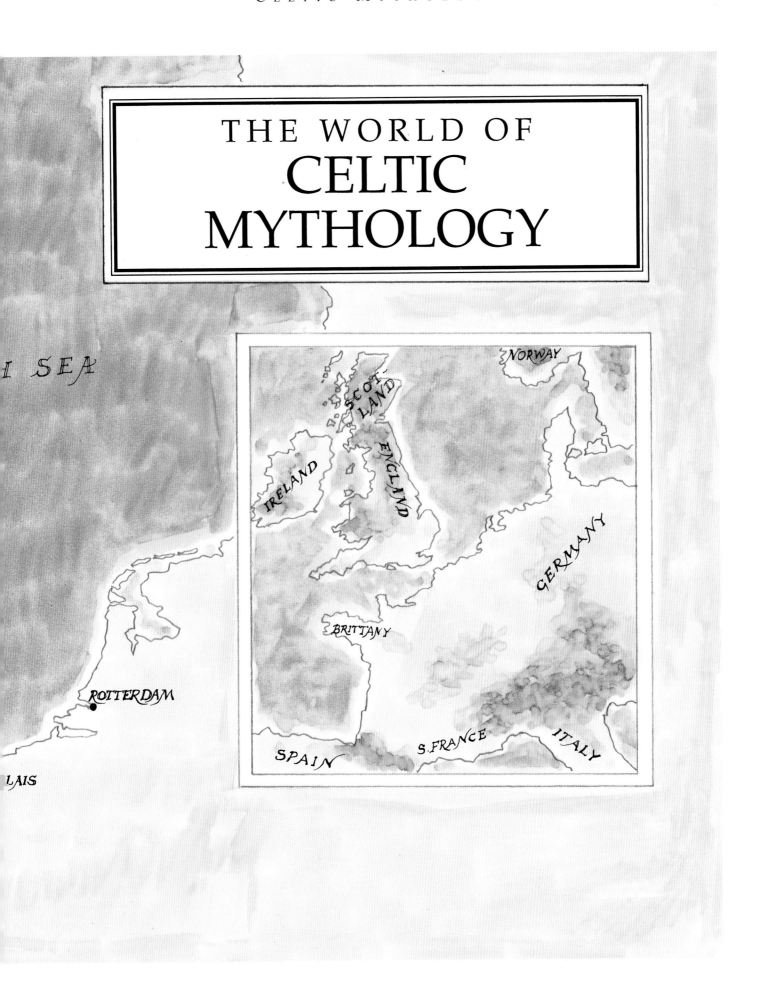

Chapter One

Who Were the Celts?

T he Celts were not a people for writing things down; they passed down their traditions and their history by word of mouth. You could say that we almost lost them in history. For people with such strong imagination and such a zest for life, they are remarkably elusive. Because they had no defined state or territory, we have to rely on what evidence they did leave behind in the form of archaeological remains, and on the record that others made of their encounters with the Celts. And for the definition of a Celt, we have to look to language more than physical remains, which is quite appropriate given the language of imagination they bequeathed us.

The Celtic People

We start with the word Celt itself, derived from the name Keltoi, given by the ancient Greeks to all those who lived north of the Alps. The underlying link of these loosely connected people was that they spoke similar languages, from the seaboard of the Atlantic as far east as India.

Left: Germans defend their land against the Romans. Some of the fiercest fights and greatest losses experienced by the Romans were with the Celts in the German forests, where the Roman formations were more susceptible to being broken by the wild charges of the enemy.

Opposite: A section of Hadrian's Wall, in Northumberland, built in the second century A.D. by the Roman Emperor Hadrian across Britain between the River Tyne and the Solway, to mark the northern limit of his Empire and to keep at bay the Celtic tribes in the far north. The final length of the Wall was 118 kilometers and was originally about 4.5 meters high, with a small fort built every Roman mile.

Above: Lia Fail inauguration stone, at the Hill of Tara, in County Meath. Tara became the sacred center of Ireland and site of the royal court of the king of Ireland. Many of the great Celtic figures are associated with Tara, from the Tuatha Dé Danaan to Cúchulainn himself. The site is on a hilltop a little over twenty miles northwest of Dublin.

Right: Dozmary Pool, in Bodmin Moor, Cornwall. Beyond the reach of the Romans, Cornwall remained a stronghold of Celtic tradition. The landscape provided inspiration for Celtic myths, which, wherever they arose, drew powerfully on the natural world and harsh but beautiful scenery around them.

Above: Roman merchants attacked by British Brigands. The trade that the Romans brought to Britain played a major role in helping to establish their position; however, since the Romans never had the long-term influence on Celtic life that they did in Gaul and elsewhere, the Celts were never fully assimilated into Roman Britain's urban life.

Two branches of the Celtic languages remain in some form: Goidelic (or Gaelic) was spoken by the earliest Celts, sometimes called Goidels, in Ireland; Brythonic or Cymric was spoken by the Brythons, or Britons. Goidelic languages survive in southern and western Ireland; in Scots Gaelic in the Scottish Highlands and the Hebrides; and in Manx, which is the old language of the Isle of Man. Brythonic or Cymric survives in contemporary Welsh; in Breton, in western Brittany; and in Cornish.

The people who spoke these languages were not one nation but loosely connected tribes that existed in Europe north of the Alps during the early centuries of the last millennium before Christ. These "Gauls" who spoke the Celtic language moved across Europe between the seventh and third centuries B.C. They spread west to the Atlantic, south into Spain, north into Britain and Ireland, and east to the Black Sea. They drew influence from these directions and exerted their own influence in return.

There were close connections between Celtic people in southern Germany and tribes in northern Italy. Some tribes settled in France; others went on to the Po Valley and, at the beginning of the fourth century, sacked Rome. But there was nothing concerted about these movements; they occurred in successive waves of tribal restlessness. The Celtic people established no cities. Their farmsteads and small hamlets were largely made of wood, wattle, and mud, easily destroyed by rival tribal raiders. They had close-knit family ties that held tribes together, but they had no administrative structure or organized state that provided any kind of permanent focus. Tribes were often at war with each other; warriors hunted and went on cattle raids, while the majority farmed cattle, pigs, and sheep, wheat and oats, or pursued their skills in ironwork and crafts.

These tribes developed common characteristics of language, art and culture, social customs, economy and way of life, and they spread widely and energetically during the fifth and fourth centuries B.C. They spread without any cohesive plan of conquest, and so the evidence of their existence is varied and ill recorded. On the mainland of Europe, they had already lost some of their initial energy by the time the Romans pushed into Gaul and Germany, just before the time of Christ, and determinedly set out to eradicate whatever remains of the Celts they found.

They survived longest in the further corners of western Europe, in Ireland and in the extremities of Britain such as Wales, Scotland, the north of England, and Cornwall in the southwest, where the Romans found it most difficult to penetrate.

Below: An army unit of Roman legionary soldiers. This re-enactment by a group known as the "Ermine Street Guard" shows clearly the ordered strength with which the largely unarmed Celts had to contend. The Celts relied on sheer courage and a fierce resolve in battle against the Romans.

Left: The Greco-Roman god Apollo was at first a god of shepherds and keeper of animals before he became also the god of the light and the sun. Roman and Greek influence often associated their own gods with those of the Celts. Some of Apollo's attributes were at times linked with those of Cernunnos (the "Horned One"), the Celtic god of the animals, who was a major figure in folklore and legend.

Whereas on the mainland of Europe the Romans firmly stamped their mark so that it survived the fall of the classical Roman Empire, they left almost no mark on the culture and life of Britain when they finally withdrew in the fifth century A.D. It was Christian, much more than Roman, influence that overtook Celtic culture in the centuries that followed.

Celtic Literature

The most dramatic evidence comes from the oral traditions of Celtic myth and legend, which were not written down until the seventh or eighth century A.D. and of which surviving versions are much later. These traditions endured mainly in Britain and Ireland and were much changed, particularly in Britain, by time and Christian influence.

Opposite: A Celtic stone head found in a field at Shipley, in West Yorkshire, England. The date is not known, but the figure shows a typical strength of character despite its simplicity. Symbolic and naturalistic heads are found all over Celtic Europe and provide us with valuable insight.

Above: The spiritual and artistic traditions of the Celts continue in these Celtic spiral stones, amulet designs based on prehistoric stone incisions (glyphs) from the sacred sites of Newgrange, Knowth and Dowth. They are hung above the Celtic Cross at Monasterboice, Ireland.

Opposite: The remains of the church and cross in the Celtic monastic settlement on the deserted island of the Skelligs, off the west coast of Ireland. Isolated sites adopted by the Celtic Christians fired the imagination and provided solitude for contemplation; they afforded some safety from raiders as well.

From Ireland, we have some of the oldest vernacular literature north of the Alps. Early Irish poetry of seventh-century poets (or fili) and eighth- and ninth-century bards was often concerned with the detail as well as the grander aspects of nature. The three main books which contain the first written record of the oral traditions of myth and legend from Celtic Ireland are the *Book of the Dun Cow*, written at the beginning of the twelfth century, the *Book of Leinster*, from the middle of the twelfth century, and the *Yellow Book of Lecan*, from the late fourteenth century.

These contain not just stories but a mixture of history, genealogy, poetry, and lore as well. They were books of education more than entertainment. For example, the *Book of Leinster* contained a full list of the stories that a trained poet was expected to know; there were 250 main tales and 100 subsidiary ones. These books themselves would have drawn on earlier manuscripts that have disappeared.

We learn about the part-mythological, part-historical ancestors of the Celts and their gods from the *Book of Invasions*, the Lebor Gabála. It has always been difficult to find any order in the structure of the Celtic gods and heroes, and this collection

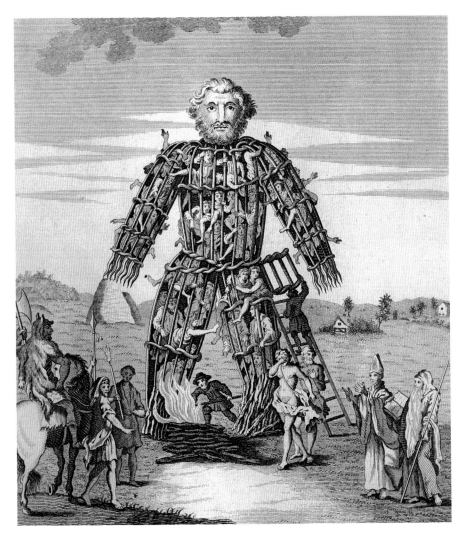

Left: The wicker man, in which captives were burned as sacrifices to Celtic gods. The Romans criticized the Celts for making human sacrifices, but had themselves stopped the practice only in quite recent history. Celtic sacrifices may not have been as common as the Romans made out, and were associated only with important ritual occasions.

was an attempt by the learned Irish of early Christian times, before the ninth century, to provide a logical explanation of the invasions of Ireland and of the Irish gods before the arrival of the Christians.

The Celts in Lore and Literature

The Roman and Greek records of the Celts is a vital part of our sketchy evidence, but we have to be wary of what the Romans wrote. They invariably cloaked Celtic gods in Roman guises. They could not recognize the beliefs of other people as beliefs which existed in their own right. The Romans were keen to absorb other cultures and to show their cultural superiority; they dismissed the Celts as barbaric, when in fact the Romans themselves had given up practices such human sacrifice only recently.

Julius Caesar spent ten years in Gaul shortly before the birth of Christ. He noted that the Gauls were devoted to their beliefs and worshiped Mercury more than any other god, followed by Apollo (god of healing), Mars (god of war), Jupiter (heavenly ruler), and Minerva (goddess of wisdom, among many other things). In Caesar's view, Mercury came closest to the typical chieftain-god of the Celts; he was accomplished in many things: inventor of the arts, the god of commerce, and the guardian of travelers.

Caesar referred to living sacrifices among the Celts and to great constructions of interwoven branches made in the form of a human body, filled with captured men,

Opposite: This ancient Celtic head was found while archaeologists were digging the various levels of the Roman temple on the grounds of Littledean Hall, in Gloucestershire, England. Roman and Celtic traditions ran closely side by side in areas of Roman colonization in Britain and Gaul. The sculptor has imbued the head with great individuality.

Right: The Bard before the Baron. *The tradition of the Celtic bard, the musician and storyteller who kept alive the myths and tales of the ancient people, continued into and beyond the Middle Ages. Here he sings in front of a Norman baron in the twelfth century.*

and set alight so that the victims died in a sea of flame. He described the common sharing of the spoils of battle and noted that heaps of spoil were to be seen piled up in sacred places; anyone who dared to hold back any spoil or take it from the pile was tortured.

The historian Tacitus, in the first century after Christ, described one of the sacred places of the Celts in North Germany. This was a sanctuary of the goddess Nerthus. He wrote of "an inviolate grove" where the goddess lived with a priest who accompanied her when she emerged from her temple in a chariot drawn by two heifers. All weapons were put away at her festival, and the people celebrated until the goddess was returned to the grove. She and her chariot were then washed in a secluded lake by slaves who disappeared afterward so that no one ever lived who had seen what happened.

Writing a little earlier in the same century, the poet Lucan also described the sacred sites that were so important to the Celts. He wrote of deep groves, solitary places, barbarous rites, and sinister worship, and he conjured up a fearful image of gloom and lifelessness in a sacred wood that Caesar had felled near Marseilles, where the altars were heaped with hideous offerings and every tree was sprinkled with human gore, and where grim images of the gods had been shaped from felled tree trunks.

Lucan also mentioned the ways in which people were sacrificed to three Celtic gods: for Tuetates, they were drowned or suffocated in a vat; for Esus, they were stabbed and then hung upon a tree; for Taranis they were burned. The Romans' highlighting of Celtic sacrifice and apparent view of it as a common and barbaric custom are probably distorted. There are many references to sacrifice and self-sacri-

Left: A granite monolith, nineteen and a half feet high, at Punchestown, County Kildare, Ireland. The Celts made their mark on the landscape with a fine dramatic sense, harmonizing with their surroundings while at the same time endeavouring to control the forces that swayed their lives.

Below: The Celtic White Horse at Uffington, in Wayland's Smithie, a 1984 painting by Gordon Wain. As symbols of wealth and power, horses were particularly important to the Celts and were sacred to the goddess Rhiannon. Above this chalk figure cut into the hillside there is also the remains of Uffington Castle, a hill fort from the Iron-Age.

fice in Celtic myth and legend, in which it is often a crucial part of the ritual expected of a chieftain and his tribe in moments of crisis. To a large extent, however, the myths themselves symbolically replaced the reality.

The Greek writer Lucian, in the second century A.D., threw quite a different light on the Celts. He told a story that underlined the value placed on poets and oratory

Right: St Michael locks the door on hell, in the form of the mouth of a whale, from an eleventh-century manuscript. Christianity imposed a vision of hell on the Celts which they themselves never had. The Underworld, or "Otherworld" was a place where the gods lived in a land of paradise and where men went to prove themselves heroes. Gods and men had a close relationship that gave added value to life in the real world.

Above: Llyn Cerrig Beach, near Valley, Anglesey, in northern Wales. Celtic artifacts found deposited in the peat here were, as in other areas rich in peat, preserved with remarkable success. We owe much of our knowledge of Celtic art to deposits of this kind, which were often ritual burial hoards.

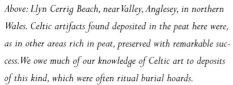

Opposite: The great chalk-cut figure of the Cerne Abbas giant, in Dorset, England, dates from Romano-Celtic times. It is 180 feet (55 meters) high and probably represents a Celtic god such as the Dagda, a father figure who was the protector of his people and a symbol of immense strength and sexual appetite.

among them. As Lucian was traveling in Gaul, he saw a picture of an old man clad in a lion skin leading a group of people whose ears were attached to his own tongue by beautiful chains of gold and amber. The men followed their leader eagerly and praised him, even though they would eventually regret the loss of their liberty. Lucian learnt that the picture represented the mighty Heracles, because the Celts believed that eloquence was more powerful than physical strength and most powerful of all in old age. Celtic chieftains relied greatly on their charisma and powers of persuasion in leading their people. Speech, adornment, weapons, and achievements won trust and loyalty, which often determined the survival of the whole tribe.

Classical writers also described great treasures of gold and silver among the Celts, and these have been found in lake sites and rivers, for example, around Toulouse. One great hoard was found in Anglesey, off the northwest corner of Wales, which was probably part of a sacrificial offering. Yet another treasure, the remarkable Gundestrup bowl with its depiction of the horned god Cernunnos, was found as a sacrificial offering buried in a bog in Jutland.

The Celts left contemporary evidence in other remains which also give solid sub-

stance to people, places, and events in the stories. There are Celtic Iron Age forts; the remains of wooden temples; ritual sites with central wooden posts; long paths bordered by statues of warriors; sanctuaries with symbolic carvings of human heads; more sophisticated statues with heads of warriors, women, and children; representations of gods and goddesses in metal, stone, and wood; and artifacts of bronze, silver and gold, often superbly made and decorated with the designs that we now readily associate with the Celts. There is even a giant naked figure wielding a club, carved in the hillside at Cerne Abbas, in Dorset, England, which may represent one of the greatest of the Celtic gods, the Dagda.

But archaeological evidence is sometimes frustrating, because the Celts were reluctant to portray their gods, just as they were reluctant, when they swore by them, to swear by their real name. "I swear by the gods by whom my people swear" was the traditional binding oath; it does not help us much in trying to identify the gods themselves.

The Celtic Mythological Cycle

The *Book of Invasions* tells how the first inhabitants of Ireland, the people of Cesair, perished in the biblical flood, all but one named Fintan. There were then six major invasions of Ireland. The first five invasions were by gods or supernatural beings; the sixth was the first invasion by humans, who ousted the old gods.

The first people to arrive in Ireland after the flood were the Fomorians (or Fomhoiré). Their name means "sea giants." The Fomorians were only half-human; they were described as hideous demons with supernatural powers, each with only one leg, one hand, one eye in the middle of the forehead, and three rows of knife-like teeth. These "original" invaders played a continuing part as resistance fighters against subsequent invasions. It is typical of the mythological and heroic tales that

Following pages: Fingal's cave on the island of Staffa in the Hebrides. This cave is made out of natural columns of rock that appear in various parts of the west coast. Understandably, the Celts and others believed the cave to have been created by giants from ancient mythology. It was the inspiration for Mendelssohn's Fingal's Cave.

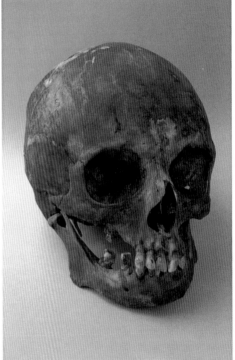

Above: Human skulls have been found buried where the Celts are supposed to have made sacrifices of their enemies in battle.

Left: An eighteenth-century allegory of the classical gods, showing them as the Celts might understand them, part of the everyday influence of the supernatural on ordinary life.

Above: The Roman god Mars on his chariot. Julius Caesar noted that the Gauls were devoted to their beliefs and that they worshipped, among others, Mars, the god of war. In their efforts to interpret and overrule Celtic myths, the Romans tended to cloak Celtic gods in Roman guise.

Right: Julius Caesar spent ten years in Gaul shortly before the birth of Christ, and we rely on his writings for much of our knowledge of the Celts at that time. This head is from a copper coin. The historian Tacitus and poet Lucian are also sources of firsthand information about the Celts, though their writings are inevitably influenced by their own bias.

enemies are portrayed as monstrous, the better to glorify those who fought and overcame them.

The next invasion occurred, with biblical precision, 268 years later, on the first of May (later to become the Celtic feast of Beltane), when a group of twenty-four men and twenty-four women landed from Spain. These bold raiders were led by Partholán, a descendant of the biblical Japheth. The Partholians, as his people were called, immediately encountered the resident Fomorians and, after desperate fighting, drove them out to the Hebrides and the Isle of Man, where the Fomorians bided their time for a comeback.

With the demonic inhabitants temporarily out of the way, the Partholians settled down and started to cultivate the soil of Ireland. At the time of their arrival, there were three lakes, nine rivers, and only one plain without trees or grass. Partholán's people set to work and cleared four more plains; they created seven new lakes; they brewed beer and introduced cattle; they were gold miners and craftspeople; they made cauldrons of metal in preference to pots of clay; they introduced laws and rituals into their society; and they had many children. Within three hundred years, there were five thousand descendants of Partholán. This assured him his place in myth as a fertility god, until disaster struck and all but one of these people were wiped out by a plague.

Thirty years later, there came the third invasion, led by Nemed mac Agnoman, with a small party of just eight people. The Nemedians at first met no resistance, there being no-one to resist them. They were able to clear more plains and create more lakes. But Nemed died and the plague returned, and so did the Fomorians.

Those Nemedians who had survived the second plague were forced to pay tribute to the Fomorians. On the first of November each year (the feast of Samhain), the Nemedians were compelled to hand over two-thirds of the children born that year and two-thirds of their corn and wine or milk. Despite bouts of brave resistance

Above: Julius Caesar invaded Britain in 55 and 54 B.C., after successful campaigns in Spain and Transalpine Gaul, but did not bring enough troops to conquer the island. It wasn't until nearly a hundred years later, in A.D. 43, during the reign of the Emperor Claudius, that the Romans first overcame the southern part of England.

and an attempted rebellion against the Fomorian stronghold, the last surviving boatload of Nemedians was forced to flee. Some went south to Spain and Greece, and some went north. Although they fled, they did not forget; they were resilient people, who took with them strong memories of the land they had lost, and descendants of both groups returned to Ireland in subsequent invasions: the southern group came back as the Fir Bolg, the northern group as the Tuatha Dé Danaan.

The Fir Bolg returned on the first of August, led by their king, Eochaid mac Eire; they came with two other groups, the Gailicendants of both groups returned to Ireland in subsequent invasions: the southern group came back as the Fir Bolg, the northern grhe Belgae, the Gauls and the Dumnonii. This puts the invasions in a historical setting. Although these invaders had been farmers in their own homes, fighting was also a way of life for them, and they developed a strong sense of loyalty to their tribal king, which set the pattern for future feuding.

The three tribes do not appear to have been much bothered by the Fomorians, who, perhaps, were developing a more philosophical outlook on the successive waves of foreigners. The tribes agreed to partition Ireland, and for a while, they lived comfortably. The Fir Bolg occupied Ulster, Munster, and Meath; the Gailiby the Fomorians, who, perhaps, were developing a more philosophical outlook on the successive waves of foreigners. The tribes agreed to partition Ireland, and for a while, they lived comfortably. omorians but by the arrival of the fifth invaders, the Tuatha Dé Danaan.

These "People of the Goddess Danu" landed, once again, symbolically, on the first of May. Led by their king, Nuada, they defeated the Fir Bolg at the First Battle of Mag Tuiredh. Eochaid was killed, and the rest of the Fir Bolg were forced to withdraw into Connacht.

The Tuatha built a new capital at Tara and tried to negotiate a peaceful settlement with the Fomorians, who had begun to take advantage of the relative chaos to re-establish themselves in a corner of Ireland. An uneasy alliance was created by the election of a new king of the Tuatha. Nuada had lost his right hand in the First Battle of Mag Tuiredh and had been forced to abdicate as a result of this physical imperfection. His successor was Bres, whose father was a Fomorian and whose mother came from the Tuatha. To set the seal on this alliance, Bres married Brigit, the daughter of one of the chieftains of the Tuatha known as the Dagda.

Bres did not live up to expectations and quickly became unpopular. He imposed

Left: Stone and Tree by Moonlight, *a 1990 pencil drawing by Godon Wain, captures the mystery of the Celtic standing stone and provides insight into the Celtic imagination.*

heavy taxes; his face became covered in boils as a result of public ridicule; and he stole the magic harp of the Dagda. When he was forced to abdicate, the truce between the Tuatha and the Fomorians was abruptly broken. The Dagda set out to retrieve his harp by diplomatic means, but the Fomorians trickily fed him a vast meal and presented him with a Fomorian maiden for the night so that he would not be able to fight. The Dagda proved himself a match for the meal and the girl, who, out of gratitude for his remarkable performance, promised to help him in the battle to come.

The Tuatha defeated the Fomorians at the Second Battle of Mag Tuiredh, when the shot from the sling of another chieftain, called Lug, hit the huge single eye of the Formorian, Balor, with such force that his head exploded and the rest of the Fomorians were routed. The stolen harp was recovered, and symbolically, the seasons were restored to their normal cycle; in turn, each aspect of Celtic mythology had its parallel in the natural world.

In the Second Battle of Mag Tuiredh, all the gods of the Tuatha gathered for the fight to reclaim Ireland from the Fomorians, and in the tales, each god is introduced with his particular skills: the smith who can forge weapons that never fail; the physician who can cure every warrior wounded in the battle; the god who supplies rivets for spears, hilts for swords, and bosses and rims for shields; and the Dagda himself, who promises "that the bones of the Fomorians under his club shall be as hailstones under the feet of herds of horses."

The final invaders were the Milesians, the first truly human warriors, who displaced the Celtic gods of the Tuatha. Their full name was the "Sons of Míl of Spain," which is where they came from. Yet again, they landed in Ireland on the feast of Beltane, the first of May, led by Amairgin, the poet, and defeated the Tuatha Dé Danaan in two separate battles. Refusing to be exiled, the Tuatha agreed to retire to the Otherworld of the prehistoric burial mounds (or *sidh*), where they became the resident Celtic gods of the pre-Christian period.

Celtic Festivals

We have seen that, in Ireland, the mythological invasion dates related to the great Celtic festivals of Samhain (November 1) and Beltane (May 1). These marked the two main divisions in the Celtic year, when the herds were brought in for the winter and when they were let out again in the spring. It was at these times that the Celts felt closest to the gods of the Otherworld.

The two other most important festivals were Imbolc (February 1) and Lugnasadh (August 1), which marked the early spring and the end of the harvest. There were regional variations on these festivals, but they had in common the major turning points of the year. They were strictly observed. The entire tribe would take part and obey the codes of behavior, to keep the peace.

The Festival of Samhain, on November 1, was the official beginning of the Celtic year and marked the onset of winter hardship. The festival has survived in the Christian world as Halloween and All Saints' Day; it is also a time to remember the dead. In Britain, the bonfires and fireworks of Guy Fawkes Night are more closely connected with this festival than with Guy Fawkes himself.

In Irish myth, Samhain was the day on which the people of Nemed had to pay the tribute of two-thirds of their corn, wine, and children to the Fomorians. This ritual signified ancient sacrifice at this time of year to appease the spirits of darkness and allay the fear that people would not survive the coming winter. Samhain was the date of the Second Battle of Mag Tuiredh, on the eve of which the Dagda mated with the goddess Morrigan, as she stood astride the River Unius, and with the god-

Above: Cupid, the Roman god of love, riding a sea monster, the symbolic form of Britain. Though the Roman presence brought peace for a while to parts of Britain, Roman soldiers were kept busy in the north and west trying to control the Celtic tribes on their borders.

Opposite: The Maypole on May Day, from the Alsace region of France. The Celtic festival of Beltane was the first of May, and marked the real beginning of summer. There were major fairs and celebrations, and the animals were purified as they left their winter quarters by passing between two fires. The tradition of the maypole is a very ancient one that has survived in modern folk custom.

dess Boann of the River Boyne, to ensure fertility in the following year.

It was a time when the doors of the sídh, the underground burial chambers, stood wide open and the gods of the Otherworld came out and played tricks on humans; many of the rituals at Samhain were intended to appease the gods. The goddess with the most influence at Samhain was the Cailleach, sometimes seen as a hag, sometimes as a mother-goddess. Samhain also marked the death of the hero Cúchulainn.

The festival of Imbolc, on February 1, was regarded as the first festival of spring. In the Celtic world, it was associated with the first lambs and the lactation of ewes, when people as well as lambs were provided with milk; this association emphasized the importance of sheep in sustaining the farming community, particularly at this time of year.

Later, the festival was taken over as the feast of St. Brigid, the Christianized version of the Celtic fertility goddess Brigid, and eventually became Candlemas. There was little celebration on this day, but it was an important milestone in the Celtic year, when the benevolent Brigid began to drive off the dark days of the Cailleach; in the Celtic perception of multiple pesonalities, the Cailleach was transformed into Brigid.

The festival of Beltane on May 1 marked the beginning of the Celtic summer, and we still give that day great seasonal and political significance. It was named after one of the most ancient and widespread of the Celtic gods, Bel, who was associated with pastoral people throughout Gaul and into northern Italy. On this day, first Partholán, then the Tuatha, and finally the Milesians landed in Ireland.

Beltane was a time of rebirth. Fires were lit the night before, and the cattle were driven between the fires in an act of ritual protection; the people danced to celebrate renewed hope and carried burning torches across the fields to encourage the sun to warm the land. Bonfires are still lit today to cleanse and purify the land and to encourage fertility. As at Samhain, the gods of the Otherworld were liable to encroach on the human world and play tricks on people.

The festival of Lugnasadh was the time to celebrate the harvest: August 1 was a fertility festival. It was also the day on which the Fir Bolg invaded Ireland and on which, symbolically, their queen, Tailtiu, died of exhaustion after clearing the land for cultivation. Tailtiu was the foster mother of Lug, after whom the festival was named. Lug was associated with games and sports, which were a major part of this and other festivals. It later became Christianized as Lammas.

Opposite: Kilclooney Moor portal tomb, near Narin, CountyDonegal. The festival of Samhain was a time when the doors of the sídh, the underground burial chambers, stood wide open. Many of the rituals at Samhain were intended to appease the gods of the Otherworld who emerged to pester or trick humans.

Left: Five of the seven planets, with Mars and Venus reconciled by Mercury. The Celtic calendar followed the movement of the moon, sun, and stars. Some of the standing stones, at Carnac in Brittany and Stonehenge in England, for example, are thought to have had astronomical significance for the Celts.

Chapter Two
Gods and Goddesses

The Celtic myth cycle centers on a rich array of gods and goddesses, existing on earth at first and later on in the "Otherworld." Their lives intertwined with one another and with those of humans, and as with Celtic festivals, many of their attributes have been absorbed into Christian imagry.

Celtic goddesses were as influential as the gods and reflected the influence of women in Celtic society; indeed, they are part of a much deeper traditional theme. As "mother-goddesses," they were mainly concerned with fertility, but they were also warriors and played a vital role in teaching the arts and secrets of war to young heroes. They also possessed magic which could determine the outcome of battle; they were shape-shifters who took other forms, such as crows or ravens, and caused fear and confusion among the enemy.

Opposite: The Giant's Causeway, County Antrim, Ireland, a wonderful example of the awe-inspiring scenery that so affected the Celtic imagination and merged, in their minds, mythology and the natural environment.

Below: Mound of the Hostages, the passage tomb from the Hill of Tara, County Meath, Ireland. It is not hard to respond to the Celtic belief that beneath such mounds lay the world of the gods and that the openings provided ways for the bold warrior to pass through to the Otherworld.

Above: An "initiate" breaking through the invisible veil separating the physical realm from the spiritual, from a seventeenth-century engraving. Although this was portrayed as a Christian illustration, it parallels the Celtic concept of easy movement between the real world and the Otherworld of the gods to which the Celtic heroes aspired.

Opposite: The goddess Rhiannon, detail from a 1984 painting by Gordon Wain. Rhiannon was the Celtic goddess of horses. She was adopted by the Romans and known as Epona in Gaul. Rhiannon was famous for her beauty; she became the wife of Pwyll and the mother of Pryderi.

Nuada

Nuada was the king of the Tuatha Dé Danaan when they invaded Ireland and defeated the Fir Bolg at the First Battle of Mag Tuiredh. As a god or chieftain, he was regarded as being almost as important as the Dagda and Lug, but there are fewer stories about him and he is less colorful than either of the other two.

Despite his magic sword, which, once unsheathed, allowed no one to escape, Nuada lost his hand in the battle and had to resign the kingship to Bres: Physical wholeness was important to the Celts. But Nuada was then fitted with an artificial arm made of silver, which earned him the name Silver Hand (Airgedlámh) and enabled him to regain the kingship after Bres was forced out. It was Nuada who finally allowed Lug to join the Tuatha Dé Danaan shortly before the Second Battle of Magh Tuiredh. Nuada acknowledged Lug's superior skills and resigned the kingship again in favor of Lug.

The Dagda

In myth, the Dagda (he is always known as "the" Dagda) was one of the great chieftains of the Tuatha Dé Danaan, but to the Celts, he was far more than that. He was

Above: Killadangan standing stones, below Croagh Patrick mountain, County Mayo, Ireland. Rising from the marshes and covered in lichen, Celtic stones like this have merged with the landscape, just as the Celtic myths have merged with the history of Ireland.

king of the Tuatha; he was Father of All (Eochaid Ollathair); he was the Lord of Perfect Knowledge (Ruad Rofhessa); he was the Dagda, the "Good God."

Following the tradition of the Celtic deities, he was master of many skills. Yet, like other Celtic gods, he also had special attributes of his own. He was god of the earth, a symbol of fertility, and he was god of wisdom, master of the science of the druids. His character was rich in contrasts that made him curiously attractive and approachable. He was portrayed as pot-bellied, ugly, and coarse; his walk was ungainly; he dressed like a peasant, with a short tunic and hood, and he wore sandals. His tunic was sometimes said to be so short that it revealed his buttocks, as a demonstration of his sexual prowess, another aspect of importance to the Celts. But he also played brilliantly on the harp, and his music helped to bring about the changing seasons of the year. He could play three special melodies on his harp: melodies that made people sleep, laugh, and grieve.

The Dagda had two wonderful possessions: a club and a cauldron. The club was a symbol of his power as the god of life and death. Eight men were needed to carry it, and he dragged it along behind him so that it created a vast rut in the ground. With the heavy end, he could kill nine men with a single blow; if he touched them with the other end, he could restore them to life again. His cauldron could never be emptied; anyone who ate from it never went away hungry. It was a symbol of life and represented the hospitality of the Celts. Both club and cauldron were powerful symbols among the Celts and among other peoples; they play important roles in the

Above: Esus, the great god of nature among the Gauls, was worshipped in the forests. This Celtic monument was discovered under the choir of Notre-dame in Paris in 1771. Esus formed a powerful triad of gods with Taranis and Teutates.

Arthurian legends, as the lance and the Holy Grail.

When the Milesians defeated the Tuatha Dé Danaan and retired them to the underground sídh, the Dagda gained a magical pig with attributes similar to those of his cauldron; the pig could be killed and eaten each day; the next day, it would come alive, ready to be killed and eaten again.

The Dagda was insatiable, as he demonstrated at the Second Battle of Mag Tuiredh when the Fomorians tried unsuccessfully to incapacitate him by forcing him to tackle a vast meal of porridge. The porridge was served from a hole in the ground that contained eighty cauldrons of milk and oats swimming with sheep, pigs, and goats. Not only did the Dagda devour this porridge greedily with a giant spoon but he wiped the hole clean with his finger so as not to waste a drop. With his belly full-stretched and his backside split through his tunic, he then so fully satisfied the woman intended by the Fomorians to exhaust him that she offered to help him in the ensuing battle.

These feats by the Dagda became part of the ritual cycle of the Celtic year. On November 1 (the feast of Samhain) each year, the Dagda was believed to unite with the goddess Morrigan, the goddess of death, on the eve of the Second Battle of Magh Tuiredh, while she stood astride the River Unius washing the armor of those who were about to die in battle. On that day, he also mated with the goddess Boann of the River Boyne, devoured the great cauldron of porridge, and mated with the daughter of the Fomorians. Through his mating with Boann, the Dagda became the

Following pages: The stillness of this Celtic landscape encapsulates the raw beauty of the natural world they inhabited. Its peacefulness contrasts with the darker, stormier aspect of the Celtic imagination. Mind and nature were two sides of the same coin.

GRANIA QUESTIONS THE DRUID

father of Aenghus mac in Og, the "young god" who is the subject of many tales.

We know that ritual offerings in the ground were a common practice in European prehistory, and it is likely that chieftains were expected to undergo comparable rituals, in a modified form, to prove their suitability as leaders and protectors of their people. The Dagda brought gods and men together by providing supernatural powers in a common, vulgar, almost humorous form that people could understand. Like the Norse god Thor, the Dagda was a god of very human appetites, but he was also a god to be respected.

Lug

Lug was the most celebrated king of the Tuatha. His character was very different from that of the Dagda; he was also far more widely celebrated. There was little cohesion in the beliefs of the Celts, but Lug comes nearest to a unifying factor, and his name appears in some form or other from Carlisle, in the north of England, to Lyons in the south of France. The Romans compared him to the god Mercury; in Wales he appears as Lleu.

Lug was young and handsome, contrasting with the coarseness of the Dagda. His name means "Shining One": He was the god of light and patron of the festival of

Above: Standing stone near Rossknowlagh, County Donegal, Ireland, catching the same light that fired the imaginations of the Celts more than two thousand years ago.

Opposite: Grania, or Gráinne, questions the old Druid about times to come, from an illustration by H.J. Ford from Andrew Lang's The Book of Romance. *The story of the elopement of Gráinne and Diarmaid is one of the most romantic and tragic in Celtic myth, and evidence of the marvelous story-telling powers of the Celtic bards.*

Right: The eagle has always been a powerful symbol in mythology, representing authority and power throughout many parts of the world. The Celts drew their inspiration from the animal world as well as from the trees and rocks around them.

Right: Celtic vampire goddess with fairies, from a 1991 watercolor painting by Wain. The concept of a powerful goddess of fertility who was an essential part of the life force as well as a goddess of death who preyed on the victims of battle was natural to the Celts.

Above: A woodland glade in West Somerset, typical of the religious sites in many parts of the Celtic lands. Not only did the woods provide sanctuary for the Druids, but the trees themselves were an important part of their worship rituals.

Lugnasadh on August 1. He was also known as Long Arm (Lámfhada) because of his use of a spear and sling, with which he could kill at great range. It was Lug who, at the Second Battle of Mag Tuiredh, slew the Fomorian champion Balor with a sling shot to his single eye and thereby won the battle for the Tuatha Dé Danaan. Lug's victory symbolized his power, for one glance from Balor's eye could kill an entire army; the victory also symbolized the victory of a new form of worship over the old gods.

Another name for Lug was the Many-Skilled (Samildánach). When the gods joined the Tuatha, each was challenged to provide a particular skill. Lug claimed first to be a carpenter but was told that the Tuatha already had a carpenter; he said he was a smith, but the Tuatha had a smith also; he claimed to be a warrior, a harpist, a poet, a historian, a hero, a physician, and a sorcerer, but the Tuatha had them all and Lug was likely to be rejected, until he claimed that no single member of the Tuatha possessed all these skills except himself, and on this basis, he was allowed to join.

This test was typical of the Celtic belief in a god, and a chieftain, who could tackle almost anything. It also showed how the Celtic gods, just like the Celtic chieftains, were expected to prove their ability to merit their position. Celtic chieftains did not take up their role by right of birth; they were elected by the people on the basis of their suitability.

There are various stories of Lug's own birth. One relates that he came from the Otherworld and had been taught his many skills by a foster father who gave him his spear, his sling, a helmet of invisibility, and a magic shield later owned by the hero

Above: The swan was an essential symbol of love to the Celtic storytellers. Aengus fell in love with the swan-maiden Caer, who, in the midst of a flock of 150 other swans, wore a golden chain and coronet .

Fin mac Cumhaill. Lug is said to have been the mythological father of the hero Cúchulainn.

Aengus mac in Og

Aengus (sometimes spelled Oengus, and the original of the modern Angus) was the son of the Dagda and the goddess Boann, spirit of the River Boyne. He is the subject of one of the best Celtic love stories. His name means "the Young One, and he was renowned for his wit and charm, though he was also a trickster. His equivalent in Wales was Mabon, and in Gaul, it was Maponos.

The birth of Aengus symbolized timelessness. His father, the Dagda, wanted to sleep with Boann, and so he sent her husband, Elcmar, on a journey under a spell that took away his sense of time and hunger. He returned nine months later, after the birth of Aengus, and imagined he had been away only a day. In later life, and with the help of the Dagda, Aengus himself tricked Elcmar out of lands that he ruled.

Aengus and the Swan Maiden

Aengus became lovesick after dreaming about a beautiful girl. He sought her with the help of his father and others and eventually discovered that she was Caer, daughter of Ethal Anubal, a prince from the sídh in Connacht. The Dagda and Aengus set out in their chariots and asked for Caer's hand. Ethal told them that Caer was more powerful than Aengus, who would have to win her without help, but Ethal was forced to reveal that his daughter spent alternate years as a woman and as a swan. Aengus found her in swan form by a lake surrounded by many other swans, each with silver chains. She promised to join Aengus if he would let her return to the lake. They embraced, fell asleep in the form of two swans, and flew around the lake three times so that he kept his promise and Caer stayed with him.

The Wooing of Édain

Midhir, the foster father of Aengus, fell passionately in love with Édain Echraidhe ("horse-riding Édain"), the beautiful daughter of King Ailill. Aengus successfully wooed Édain, on behalf of Midhir, but not surprisingly, Midhir's first wife, Fuamhnach, who had trained with a druid, was so jealous that she struck Édain with a rowan stick and turned her into a pool of water, which first became a worm and then an incredibly large and beautiful fly (or butterfly).

Midhir continued to take so much pleasure in the fly that Fuamhnach created a wind to blow Édain around the world until she came to the house of Aengus, who placed her in a crystal bower filled with marvelously scented plants and herbs and carried her with him wherever he went. Learning of this, Fuamhnach lured Aengus from his house and sent another wind that blew Édain out of her sanctuary, over Ireland, down the smoke hole of the warrior Édar, and into the wine cup of his wife, who swallowed the fly. Édain was reborn as this woman's human daughter and was brought up by Édar.

Meanwhile the king of Ireland, Eochaid Airemh, sent messengers throughout the land in search of a wife; he heard of the beauty of Édar's daughter, rode to find her, payed the bride price, and took her home, where his brother, Ailill, also fell secretly, and incestuously, in love with Édain. Ailill did not confess his love until Eochaid went on a tour of Ireland and, in his absence, left Édain in Ailill's care. Pestered by Ailill, Édain finally agreed to have a tryst with him if he would then leave her alone, but Ailill wasted his opportunity. For three nights in succession, he slept throughout the night instead of keeping the tryst, and Édain dreamed of a stranger instead.

On the third night of her dream, the stranger confessed that he was Midhir, who had heard of her beauty and recognized her as the wife he had lost to Fuamhnach's jealousy. He begged Édain to go away with him, but she refused to do so without the permission of her new husband, Eochaid. On his return home, Eochaid deviously agreed to give up Édain if Midhir could beat him at chess. Midhir let Eochaid win the first game and, as forfeit, built a great causeway across the bogs of Meath.

Midhir then won the second chess match, but when he returned to claim his prize, Eochaid had barred the doors of Tara and sat feasting with his warriors inside. Undeterred, Midhir used his supernatural powers to enter the hall and seize Édain. They flew together, in the form of two swans, up through the smoke hole of the hall.

Eochaid and his warriors pursued Midhir and started to dig up the sídh where he lived, until Midhir promised to return Édain if Eochaid could identify her out of fifty replicas. Eochaid thought that an easy test and immediately chose the version who had been the original daughter of Ailill, rather than the Édain who had been reborn as the daughter of Édar. Midhir kept the real Édain, and they had a son, the

Following pages: The Aran Island cliffs at Inishmore, off the west coast of Ireland, drop straight into the sea. The three islands that make up the Arans are bare and treeless with little soil, yet around one thousand people still live there, fishing and farming, following a lifestyle that their Celtic ancestors might well have recognized.

Above: The great Celtic feast days were times for celebration and drinking, for letting go the hardships of everyday life. Beer was the most common drink, though the aristocracy enjoyed wine imported from the Mediterranean.

Above right: The Sea Maiden, a frontispiece illustration by John Batten from Joseph Jacob's Celtic Fairy Tales, 1892. The nineteenth century was a time for great collections of ancient legend and folklore, often based on very thorough research, which provided the basis for much of our present-day knowledge.

hero Conaire Meplicas. Eochaid thought that an easy test and immediately chose the version who had by ever after.

Danu

Tuatha Dé Danaan means "People of the Goddess Danu." Danu was the daughter of the Dagda and spoken of as the mother of several other gods, but like those of so many of the Celtic gods, her identity and relative status are not always clear. Sometimes she was equated with the benevolent Brigid, who was worshiped more widely than Danu; sometimes, with the less benevolent Anu, whose name survives in the hills shaped like a woman's breasts and known as the Paps of Anu in County

Kerry, Ireland. This triple identity is typical of Celtic thinking and underlines Danu's role as a mother-goddess with a range of responsibilities.

Brigid

The goddess Brigid was one aspect of the mother-goddess Danu, but she also had an important role as queen or goddess of the northern British tribe of the Brigantia. The Romans associated her with Minerva. Caesar wrote that she was the patron of the arts and crafts; the Romans also believed her to have healing powers, and she became associated with healing wells and springs, and with fertility, childbirth, and maternity. A Roman statue of the third century B.C., in Dumfries, Scotland, shows her in her role of queen, holding a spear and globe and with wings of victory on her shoulders. She survived as St. Brigid in the Christian calendar and continued her association with learning and culture.

Macha

The goddess Macha was another warrior queen, who forced the sons of her enemies to build the ancient capital of Ulster, Emain Macha, the "Brooch of Macha." She was also a mother-goddess. There was a story that, when she was pregnant, she was forced to race against the horses of the Ulster king, Conchobar mac Nessa. She won the race, but the exertion brought on the birth of her twins and caused her death. Before she died, she put a curse on the men of Ulster: For nine generations

Below: The entrance to Wayland's Smithy, a burial mound in Oxfordshire, England, typical of the solidly constructed burial places in which the aristocratic Celts expected to withdraw to an eternal afterlife of pleasure and reward. The care with which they provided for their death rivaled that of many more sophisticated cultures.

they would suffer the pangs of childbirth for five days and four nights in the hour of their greatest need. Macha became the goddess of games and festivals and was the horse goddess in the guise of Epona. She was also one of the forms of the goddess Morrigan.

Morrigan

Morrigan was the goddess of death, but also of sexuality, war, and fertility. With her red hair and demonic energy, she had a formidable reputation as a powerful influence on the lives of the Celts. Her name means "Phantom Queen." When she mated with the Dagda on the eve of the Second Battle of Mag Tuiredh, she was washing the bloodied bodies and armor of those about to die in the battle, but this mating was also symbolic of fertility for the river and the land, as well as for those warriors who would replace the dead.

Morrigan, like Danu, had a triple identity, consisting of Macha; Nemhain, which means "frenzy;" and Badba, which means "crow" or "raven." In that form, she was often seen as a bird flying over the battlefield, selecting her victims; she also appeared in the form of a hag or, sometimes, as a beautiful and seductive maiden. Morrigan was a prophetess of doom but she was also the life force that drove warriors on to greater achievements.

The Celtic Otherworld

After their defeat by the Milesians at the Second Battle of Mag Tuiredh, the gods of the Tuatha withdrew from the upper world of Ireland. Some went underground to take possession of the natural burial mounds of ancient Ireland, the sídh, where they ruled a supernatural world of their own. Others went overseas to the Land under the Waves (Tír fTuatha withdrew from the upper world of Ireland. Some went underground to take possession of the natural burial mounds of ancient Ireland, the s sea.

In the Celtic imagination, the Otherworld was a promised land that warriors and common people yearned for as reward for the hardship of life; it was a land of great happiness where time had no meaning and mortal perfection was realized; the land was rich and the living easy; there was feasting and music and lovemaking; and though there was still plenty of fighting, wounded warriors always recovered to fight again. A year in a sídh might be the equivalent of several centuries or only a few minutes in the human world. This unknown factor made the exploits of heroes even more heroic.

The line of demarcation between the real world and the Otherworld was often blurred. Human heroes might enter the Otherworld by invitation of the gods who lived there, to help them against a rival sídh in return for the love of a goddess; sometimes the humans would enter by force, to steal a treasure of the gods that might benefit humans. In the legends, heroes were allowed to move freely among historical figures and among the gods and goddesses, all in the same story. Here is a symbol of the transition of the Celts from the ancient mythical world to a world where humans had more control, a slow process in which Christianity also played a part.

The Celtic Underworld was different from the Otherworld; it was a place of phantoms and fear, the haunt of the sorceress Scáthach and the giant Yspaddaden, where heroes went to prove their courage in order to earn the rewards of the Otherworld.

Conn of One Hundred Battles

The Otherworld represented everything the Celtic heart might desire. This was reflected in the story of Conn Cétchathlach (Conn of One Hundred Battles), grandfather of Cormac mac Airt.

Conn stood one day on the ramparts of Tara with his druids and poets, watching a horseman approach out of the swirling mists. The horseman invited Conn to accompany him to his home, which had a golden ridgepole and was built next to a golden tree. Inside there was a girl sitting on a crystal chair, wearing a golden crown, and nearby her were a silver vat and a golden cup and bowl. The girl represented the Sovereignty of Ireland and served Conn with meat and ale.

The great god Lug himself was there, sitting on a throne, having returned after his death to tell Conn how long he would reign. When the vision faded, Conn was left with the silver and gold and a yew branch on which the names of his successors had been written.

Cormac's Vision

A similar vision of the Otherworld also appeared to Conn's grandson, Cormac mac Airt, who is supposed to have been a historical king of Ireland in the third century, and who died from a salmon bone stuck in his throat.

Cormac, too, stood on the ramparts of Tara when he was visited by Manannán mac Lir (the son of Lir, god of the sea), who had come to show Cormac the Land of Promise. Manannán, in disguise, described a land where there was only truth, where there was no old age nor decay nor sadness nor envy nor jealousy nor hatred nor arrogance. He persuaded Cormac to grant him three wishes in exchange for three golden apples on a branch that Manannán carried; when the branch was shaken, the apples made enchanting and healing music.

A year later, Manannán, no longer in disguise, claimed his three wishes and took away Cormac's son, daughter, and wife. Cormac pursued him, became lost in a mist, and discovered a wonderful palace, where he was welcomed and feasted by a handsome warrior and a beautiful girl. Cormac's family was restored to him, and all returned home, together with the golden apples and a magical golden cup which broke into three pieces whenever three lies were spoken over it and was restored whenever three truths were spoken.

The Cauldron of Plenty was often seen as a symbol of the Otherworld and is reflected in the endless search for the Holy Grail in the Arthurian legends.

Opposite: Beltany stone circle, near Raphoe, County Donegal, Ireland. Stone circles were religious sites and sometimes defensive ones as well. They mark the landscape indelibly and are likely to withstand all that nature can throw at them for another two or three thousand years.

Left: Newgrange passage grave with standing stone at County Meath, Ireland. One of the most perfectly preserved burial mounds, it is remarkable for the labor involved in building it and for the confidence that inspired it.

Chapter Three
The Great Celtic Heroes

Not all the heroes and heroines of Celtic mythology were superhuman. The greatest heroes of Celtic lore were the warriors, heroes such as Cúchulainn and Fin mac Cumhaill. Though Cúchulainn and Fin mac Cumhaill were human, they did possess super-human qualities. Cúchulain was reputed to be the son of a god, and legend has it that Fin mac Cumhaill lived to be 230 years old. Their names are more widely known than any god or goddess in Celtic mythology, and both heroes are still honored by Celtic people today.

Opposite: Clwy Llangollen Castell, Dinas Bran, the landscape in which the great Welsh Celtic legends grew and took hold of the imagination.

Below: A painting of the ruins of Tintagel Castle, Cornwall, from early in the twentieth century. Tintagel was said to have been the birthplace of King Arthur, whose adventures, and those of his knights, are a complex mixture of pagan and Christian traditions.

The Hero Cúchulainn

Cúchulainn was the epitome of Celtic valor, the defender of his tribe, the ideal chieftain who used his extraordinary powers solely for the benefit of his people, and a bridge between the worlds of gods and humans; he is also the foremost hero in the collection of stories known as the Ulster Cycle. Cúchulainn was based at the royal court of Chonchobar mac Nessa, at Emain Macha, and the stories are set at some time before the third century A.D.

He was reputed to be the son of the god Lug; his mother was Deichtine, the daughter (or sister) of Chonchobar, the king. In looks and stature, he was very different from his fellows; he was small and dark, with no beard, among people who were taller, fair, and bearded. These characteristics marked him out historically as a foreigner. His original name was Sédanta, which linked him to the British tribe of the Setanti, whose tribal hero he may have been.

Cúchulainn was brought up in the typical manner of a high-born Celt: He was fostered out to Amairgin, the poet, and educated by the historian Sencha in wisdom, the warrior Fergus in warfare, and the druid Cathba in magic; he was also taught by the sorceress Scáthach, who became his mistress and the mother of his son Conall. One of Cúchulainn's tragedies was that he killed Conall in a fight, without realizing who he was fighting.

Cúchulainn's battle frenzies were renowned. His features became utterly distort-

Above: Buried wedge tomb, at Inishowen, County Donegal, Ireland. Through these entrances to the Otherworld, the Celtic heroes such as Cúchulainn entered to mingle with the gods and goddesses, often at their requests for help. Celtic kings and heroes were held responsible by the people for protecting them from the gods as much as from their mortal enemies.

Opposite: The hero Cúchulainn with Morrigan, the goddess of death, who appeared in the guise of a black carrion crow, the bird of the battlefields, from an illustration by Bestall, c.1928. In such a guise, Morrigan flew around Cúchulainn at the time of his death at the hands of his enemies.

ed. He turned round in his skin so that his feet and knees faced backward and his
calves and buttocks faced forward; his long hair stood on end, with a spot of blood
or a spark of fire on each tip; fire blazed from his mouth, and from the top of his
head shot up a spout of dark blood as high as the mast of a ship; one eye sank deep
into his skull, and the other protruded onto his cheek. He wielded a terrible barbed
spear, the *gae bolga*, which he flung with invincible result, from between his toes.
These berserk fits, accompanied by the single eye, puts him in the same tradition as
the Viking hero Egill Skallagrimson or even the Norse god Odin himself. In his state
of rage, Cúchulainn could be pacified only by being plunged into three successive
vats of cold water.

Sédanta earned his later name, Cúchulainn, or Hound of Culann, when at the age
of about seven he was attacked by the fierce hound belonging to the smith Culann.
Cúchulainn killed the hound by throwing his ball down its throat and dashing out its
brains on a rock. When Culann complained at the loss of his hound, Cúchulainn

*Opposite: Cúchulainn in battle, attended by Morrigan, the
goddess of death, in the form of a crow. Wealthy Celtic warriors rode into battle in chariots, making occasional charges
and hurling their lances. They would then descend for hand-
to-hand fighting. Cúchulainn's battle frenzies were renowned;
his entire physique became distorted as his fury grew.*

agreed to act as watchdog until Culann trained another dog to take his place. The symbolic meaning that lay behind this tale was that Cúchulainn would guard the kingdom of Ulster and protect its people.

There was another price he had to pay. Offered by the gods the chance of a long life or fame, he chose fame and was bound by a magical obligation (or *geis*) never to pass a hearth without tasting food and never to eat the flesh of a dog. He was warned that his first and last actions would be the killing of a dog.

The Cattle Raid of Cualnge

The Taín bó Cualnge (or Cattle Raid of Cooley) is probably the most famous of Cúchulainn's exploits in the rivalry between the provinces of Connacht and Ulster. On account of a quarrel with her husband, Ailill, Queen Medb of Connacht set out to steal the Brown Bull of Cualnge from Ulster. Tales of cattle raids were common among warlike people who lived off cattle rearing, and such myths also appear among the ancient stories of Greece, India, and elsewhere.

Queen Medb reviewed her army in preparation for the attack on Ulster; each section of the army appeared more magnificent than the last as the march-past

Above: Replica of King Arthur's sword at Taunton Castle in Somerset, England. Legend has it that whoever could draw the magic sword from the stone would win the right to become king of England. As a young man Arthur drew the sword, where no other knight had been able to do so.

Opposite: Cúchulainn asks King Conor for arms. The Celtic heroes such as Cúchulainn possessed remarkable powers, but were still subservient to the king and owed him allegiance. Much of the tension in the legends is created by the conflict of interests between the hero's loyalty to his king and to his friends.

THE DEATH OF DIARMID

Diarmid Seizes The Giant's Club

Opposite: The death of the Celtic hero Diarmaid, an illustration by H.J. Ford from Andrew Lang's The Book of Romance. *The story of Diarmaid and Grainne ends tragically when Diarmaid is mortally wounded and Fin mac Cumhaill betrays him by letting the life-giving water that Diarmaid needs slip through his fingers, thereby causing the hero's death.*

Left: Diarmaid, fighting with the giant, seizes his club in an illustration by H.J. Ford from Andrew Lang's The Book of Romance. *The story is more than one of daring deeds. It draws richness from the dilemma that Diarmaid faces in allowing himself to be seduced by Grainne, who was already betrothed to the aging Fin mac Cumhaill, of whom Diarmaid was a loyal subject.*

reached its climax with the appearance of her champion, Cormac. Such a buildup was typical of the greatest heroic legends, among the Norsemen and the Persians, and even with Charlemagne.

Medb's campaign started off well, when she found the Ulstermen under the vengeful curse of the goddess Macha that made them as weak as a woman in labor for five days and four nights in moments of crisis. Only Cúchulainn was strong enough to fight and so, with his charioteer, he took up his position at a ford to defend Ulster.

Medb sent her bravest heroes, one by one, to attack Cúchulainn, but each was slain until, finally, she sent Ferdia, who had grown up with Cúchulainn as his foster brother under the tutelage of Scáthach. Ferdia refused to fight until Medb shamed him and Cúchulainn into a reluctant but tremendous battle. Having learned the art

Previous pages: Glastonbury Tor, in Somerset, England, where sixth-century occupation has been found contemporary with the dates attributed to King Arthur. Glastonbury is also known as the "Isle of Avalon." It is supposed to be the final burial place of Arthur.

of fighting from the same person, they battled for three days and embraced each other at the end of each of the first two days. On the third day, Cúchulainn built up one of his rages (riastrad) and mortally wounded Ferdia with his barbed spear (gae bolga). Once more, he embraced Ferdia and carried him with his weapons across the ford to the Ulster side, where he mourned the death of his friend. Their fight symbolized the conflict between a warrior's duty to his lord and the duties of kinship and comrades, a continual tension among the tribal Celts.

While the fighting at the ford was at its height, and the men of Ulster slept, the men of Connacht slipped in and stole the Brown Bull of Cualnge. Too late, King Chonchobar and the Ulstermen awoke and drove Queen Medb and her warriors home. There, she gained little pleasure from her capture of the Brown Bull, which ran riot around the countryside and, in another tremendous fight, killed the White Bull of Connacht. Medb ended up without either bull, and peace was patched up again, but only for a short time.

The Death of Cúchulainn

Cúchulainn was invincible in battle under normal circumstances, but he was not invulnerable. It was important to the Celts that their chieftains and heroes triumph over their enemies and also be human. Cúchulainn died eventually, defeated only by supernatural powers that he could not be expected to withstand.

Once again, Queen Medb of Connacht attacked, seeking to destroy Cúchulainn with the help of specially trained sorcerers. On the eve of battle, the hero passed

Above: Tintagel, in Cornwall, was the site of an early sixth-century Celtic monastery as well as the supposed birthplace of King Arthur.

Opposite: The surviving church tower on Glastonbury Tor, the site of an early Celtic monastery and supposed last resting place of King Arthur.

Left: Merlin, the magician of the Arthurian tales, enchanted by Vivien, an illustration by Arthur Rackham. King Arthur relied greatly on the skills and good counsel of Merlin, part of whose charm is his own susceptibilities.

Above: Moloch, the demon god to whom the Ammonites are supposed to have sacrificed children. Human beings are represented as being shut up in the cells within the body of the model and burned to death by the fires below. This seventeenth-century woodcut is reminiscent of the wicker man supposedly used by the ancient Celts for sacrifice.

the sorcerers as they were roasting a dog at a hearth. Obedient to his geis, or fatal obligation, he stopped at the hearth to taste the food, and he let himself be persuaded to break his taboo against eating dog. His powers were immediately weakened, and in the ensuing fight, known as the Great Carnage of Mag Muirthemne, he was mortally wounded.

Cúchulainn promptly succumbed to his fate again. He washed himself in the river and killed an otter that drank the blood-stained water. Remembering it had been prophesied that his first and last actions would be the killing of a dog (the Hound of Culann and the water-dog, the otter), he realized that his end had come. In his death agony, Cúchulainn bound himself to a stone pillar, defied his enemies, and so died with honor intact. When his foes saw three crows light on Cúchulainn's head, they knew that Morrigan, the goddess of death, had come in her three guises to claim him, so they marched up and cut off his head.

Fin mac Cumhaill

Whereas Cúchulainn was the symbol of a great leader within the tribal system, Fin (or Fionn) mac Cumhaill was the heroic outsider, who led a band of warriors known as the *fian*. Fin is the central character in the collection of stories known as the Fenian or Ossianic Cycle, named after his son, Ossian (or Oisin), one of the

Opposite: Arthur and Mordred in mortal combat, an illustration by Arthur Rackham. While Arthur was fighting on the mainland of Europe, his nephew Mordred traitorously seized the crown and Arthur's wife, Queen Guinevere. In the ensuing battle, both Mordred and Arthur were killed.

most famous Celtic poets. The Ossianic Cycle is later than Cúchulainn's Ulster Cycle. Fin means "fair," the fair son of Cumhaill, and he, too, was a poet. He is said to have died at the age of 230 years, in about the third century A.D., and was a contemporary of King Cormac mac Airt.

Fin and his roving band typified the groups of young warriors who for various reasons could not fit into the pattern of tribal life; they became a mercenary force without immediate tribal obligations, fighting for whoever needed them at the time, and occupied with hunting and raiding between the conflicts. He maintained a much stronger hold on the imagination of the common people than did Cúchulainn, helped by the popularity of stories about him that had a wider appeal.

Many of Fin's exploits are concerned with magic and are closely connected with the Celtic Otherworld, where Fin sometimes fought on the side of the gods. He and his warriors were renowned for their bravery and skill in battle and also for the cultural arts. Fin was chosen as their leader not for his great physical qualities but because of his wisdom, truthfulness, and generosity. Like Cúchulainn, and despite his supernatural powers, Fin was mortal. He is often associated with his two hounds, Bran and Sgeolan; these happened to be his nephews, whose mother, the sister of Fin's wife, had been turned into a wolfhound.

Diarmaid and Grainne

This is one of the best-known romantic tales involving Fin mac Cumhaill. In later life, after a number of marriages, he wished to marry Grainne, the daughter of the king, Cormac mac Airt, but like many maidens in Celtic tales, she had other ideas.

Above: Burial mounds under snow at Priddy in Somerset, England. The Celtic winter was harsh, a time to gather around the fire for storytelling about the gods who lived in the Otherworld beneath the mounds.

Opposite: The baby Arthur is discovered by Merlin on the beach at Tintagel. Arthur was the illegitimate son of Uther Pendragon, King of England, and Igerna, wife of the Duke of Cornwall. It was Merlin who helped Uther disguise himself as Igerna's husband and enter her bedroom. Arthur was subsequently brought up under Merlin's tutelage.

O YOUNG MARINER,
DOWN TO THE HAVEN,
CALL YOUR COMPANIONS,
LAUNCH YOUR VESSEL,
AND CROWD YOUR CANVAS.
AND ERE IT VANISHES
OVER THE MARGIN,
AFTER IT, FOLLOW IT,
FOLLOW THE GLEAM."

MERLIN AND THE GLEAM
TENNYSON

At their wedding feast, she drugged Fin's wine and that of his warriors and ran off with the hero of her choice, Fin's nephew, Diarmaid ua Duibhne.

To give him his due, Diarmaid was reluctant at first, because of his loyalty to Fin, but in Irish legends, the love of the lady is invariably the stronger force. Despite imploring Grainne to stay with Fin, he was seduced by her magic powers and her beauty; they escaped while Fin slept, and when Grainne became tired, Diarmaid carried her in his arms.

When Fin awoke, he sent his warriors after the couple, but for once, Fin's men were more loyal to their comrade Diarmaid than to their lord, and they helped him evade pursuit. Fin himself pursued the couple into the woods. While Grainne was taken to safety by Diarmaid's foster father, Aengus mac in Og, Diarmaid performed amazing feats of bravery to hold Fin at bay.

After such a show of valor, Diarmaid was unable to resist Grainne, despite his best intentions, and he became her lover. Through the efforts of Aengus, Fin seemed reconciled to losing Grainne but continued to desire her. While pretending to be friendly, he plotted his revenge.

Diarmaid was invited to a boar hunt, during which he was gored by a supernatural boar. He begged Fin to bring him a drink of water to quench his intolerable thirst. Fin brought water from the brook in his cupped hands but let the water slip through his fingers; he went back for more water, and the same thing happened; the third time, he took pity on Diarmaid and brought the water safely to him. It was too late. Diarmaid was dead. The amoral nature of Celtic legends is highlighted in Fin's subsequently forcing Grainne to marry him. There are similarities between the conflicts of loyalty in this legend and in the legend of Tristan and Isolde.

Opposite: Merlin and the "Gleam," from the illumination by E.F. Beckett. The text reads:

> *"O young mariner,*
> *Down to the haven,*
> *Call your companions,*
> *Launch your vessel*
> *And crowd your canvas,*
> *And ere it vanishes*
> *Over the margin,*
> *After it, follow it,*
> *Follow the Gleam."*

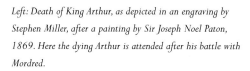

Left: Death of King Arthur, as depicted in an engraving by Stephen Miller, after a painting by Sir Joseph Noel Paton, 1869. Here the dying Arthur is attended after his battle with Mordred.

Chapter Four
The Mabinogion

The other body of literature that survives from the Celtic period is from Britain, in particular from Wales, where there were similar oral traditions that did not begin to be written down until long after the period of the Celts themselves. The work of Welsh poets such as Taliesin and Aneirin, from the sixth and seventh centuries A.D., were not transcribed until the ninth or tenth centuries, and books of their poems do not survive from earlier than the thirteenth century. The oldest Welsh manuscript is the *Black Book of Camaerthen*, from the late twelfth century.

The stories in British myth and legend were not written down until several centuries after the Irish legends were first transcribed. The Welsh stories still have a Celtic flavor, but they have been rewritten by Christian influence. They belong, quite simply, to another age; they are medieval rather than pagan. Often it is magic rather than heroics that facilitates success.

The Mabinogion is a collection of Welsh tales that go back to some of the earliest Celtic legends. Mabinogi literally means "instruction for young poets." The collec-

Opposite: The Poulnabrone Dolmens, County Clare, Ireland. Celtic stones in all their forms—dolmens, cromlechs, circles and pillars—still bring an air of mystery to the landscape wherever the Celts were established.

Left: A cross slab, The Burren, in County Clare, Ireland. Christianity also made its mark in stone , and is more prevalent in the Welsh legends than in those of Ireland.

tion was put together by Lady Caroline Guest in the mid-ninteenth century and was drawn largely from two manuscripts of the fourteenth and fifteenth centuries, which were themselves compilations of much earlier Celtic supernatural and magical tales. These were the *Red Book of Hergest* and the *White Book of Rhydderch*.

Four of the best-known Mabinogi are contained in the *Red Book of Hergest*. They are known as the Four Branches: the stories of Pwyll, prince of Dyved; Branwen, daughter of Llyr; Manawyddan, son of Llyr; and Math, son of Mathonwy. All four tales are to some extent connected, and the hero Pryderi, son of Pwyll, appears in three of them.

Not surprisingly, there is a central theme of strife that runs through the tales: the conflict between the Children of Don and the Children of Llyr. The Children of Don include Ludd, or Nudd, a ruler with a silver hand, to compare with the Irish Nuada; Gwydion; Llew Llaw Gyffes; and Arianrod. The Children of Llyr include Llyr, his son Manawyddan, and Bran the Blessed (Bran means "raven"). There have been suggestions that the Children of Llyr were gods of the Underworld, whereas the Children of Don were sky gods, and that their ongoing strife represented the rivalry between successive gods worshiped in Britain.

Pwyll, Prince of Dyved

Pwyll temporarily changes shape with the king of Annwyn (Hades) in order to win Rhiannon, a fertility goddess, as his wife, although she was betrothed to Gwawl

Opposite: Detail of the painting Country Magic, *1984, by Gordon Wain. Celtic myth was closely tied in with the natural environment, especially birds, animals, and vegetation; these connections between the spirits and nature have survived in folklore.*

Left: The Roman god Pan, half-man and half-goat, was also known to the Celts and closely associated with the natural world, particularly with the trees and forests that were so important to the Celts.

Right: Herefordshire Beacon hillfort, in the Malvern Hills, close to the border between England and Wales. The Welsh tribes defended themselves steadfastly against the invading Romans, who found it more difficult to conquer in the west than they had in the south. Wales became a Celtic stronghold, and poetry and legend flourished there.

(whose name means "light"). Pwyll tricked Gwawl by enticing him into a bag and freeing him on condition that he gave up Rhiannon. The son of Pwyll and Rhiannon was Pryderi, who vanished soon after his birth, reappeared several years later, and became Lord of the Underworld.

Bran and Branwen

Branwen, the daughter of Llyr, the sea god, and sister of Bran, was married to the king of Ireland, Matholwch, who came to Wales to claim her. During his visit, Matholwch was insulted, refused to accept compensation offered by Bran, and returned to Ireland with Branwen, who then received rough treatment in revenge for the insult.

In the resulting war, both the Irish and British armies suffered terrible losses. Bran was wounded in the foot with a poisoned arrow which caused him such terrible pain that he ordered his head to be cut off and buried in the White Mound, in London, with its face toward France. As long as the head was undisturbed, so ran the legend, Britain would never be invaded. Bran joined the roll call of leaders who sacrificed themselves for their people, and Branwen herself died of grief and was buried in Anglesey.

Bran was described as a king of Britain, but he was clearly also a god with supernatural powers. He was so huge that no house could be built that was big enough for him; and he was equally strong. He had magical gifts, including a cauldron which came originally from Ireland and which he returned as a gift to Matholwch in an attempt to pacify him; the cauldron could restore the dead to life, but without the power of speech. When Bran was forced to fight Matholwch, he waded across the Irish Sea with his mountainous body; when he laid himself down across a river, a whole army could march across his back. But in the tradition of Celtic heroes and gods, he was also a cultured poet, a patron of the arts, and a skilled harpist.

Manawyddan, Son of Llyr

In the story of Manawyddan, the last surviving child of Llyr, he and Pryderi team up to endure a barrage of evils inflicted on them in vengeance for the treatment of Gwawl by Pryderi's father, Pwyll. Manawyddan was a shadowy god of fertility and crafts. His fortress in Gower was reputed to have been built of human bones, in a reference to sacrifice practiced by the early Celts.

Math, Son of Mathonwy

Math was a wizard in a family famed for magic. His story mainly concerns his nephews, Gwydion and Gilfaethwy, who first tricked Pryderi and then waged war with him until he was killed. In Math's tale also, Llew Llaw Gyffes was born and married the beautiful, sweet-scented Blodeuwedd, who betrayed her husband and was turned into an owl.

Gwydion

Gwydion was skilled in war and in the arts of peace, poetry, eloquence, and magic; he is a warrior god and a father figure in Welsh mythology. Gwydion and his brother, Gilfaethwy, were the nephews of Math, son of Mathonwy, a famous magician who had instructed them both in sorcery.

One of Math's peculiarities was that he had always, except in time of war, to have a virgin by him to hold his feet in her lap. Gilfaethwy fell in love with Math's foot holder, the virgin Goewin, a girl of exceptional beauty and virtue. Gwydion promised to help his brother outwit their uncle and win the girl, which proved to be a complicated venture.

Setting about the task in a roundabout way, Gwydion offered to obtain for Math the wonderful swine which belonged to Pryderi, ruler of Dyved. Disguised as a bard, with Gilfaethwy and some companions, Gwydion went to Pryderi's court, where he was welcomed because of his magnificent storytelling, on account of which Pryderi agreed to exchange the swine for a gift of twelve stallions, twelve greyhounds, and twelve golden shields, which Gwydion had secretly created by magic.

Gwydion and Gilfaethwy hurried away with the swine before Pryderi discovered that his magical gift had evaporated into nothing. Determined not to be so easily cheated, Pryderi pursued the brothers, at which point Math marched out to confront Pryderi in their defense.

This confrontation created the opportunity toward which Gwydion had been deviously working. With their uncle gone to war, the brothers slipped back to Math's court, both raped Goewin in Math's own bed, and then returned to the battle, where Math agreed that the outcome should be decided by single combat, in which Gwydion used his magic powers to kill Pryderi.

Llew Llaw Gyffes

Llew has been compared with the Irish chieftain-god Lug and, like him, carried a spear and sling. His story in the Mabinogion follows on from that of Gwydion, with more trickery, passion, force, and deceit.

After the death of Pryderi, Math punished his nephews, Gwydion and Gilfaethwy, for the rape of his foot holder, the virgin Goewin. He then subjected their sister, Arianrod, to a chastity test to see if she might be a suitable successor to Goewin.

Above: Brigid's Well, near Kildare, Ireland. St Brigid was the Christianized version of the old Celtic goddess, Brighid, who in all her three forms was the daughter of the Dagda. The early Christian monks, seeking to convert the tribesfolk, were adept at translating Celtic myths and gods into Christian terms.

Opposite: Celtic interlace patterns from the painting Bryn Kellydee, Angelesey, *1985, by Gordon Wain. The typical geometric patterns found on Celtic artifacts have remained a powerful inspiration to artists today.*

But Gwydion was guilty of incest as well as rape, and Arianrod failed the test when, as she left the room where Math was quizzing her, she dropped a boy child and "another bundle." Gwydion snatched up the bundle (the result of his incestuous relationship) before anyone saw it and hid it in a chest.

Gwydion brought the child up and took him, as a young boy, to meet his mother. Arianrod was not pleased at being reminded of the result of her shameful union, and she made three vows. First, she refused Gwydion's request to give the boy a name. Gwydion vowed that she would and tricked her into doing so. When Arianrod saw the boy, in disguise, hit a wren at some distance, she said that he had a fair and deft hand; from that, he took his name, Llew of the Strong Hand. Her second vow was that the boy would never bear arms until she herself armed him. Again Gwydion tricked her into going against her vow.

Arianrod's third vow was that Llew would never have a mortal wife, but with the help of his uncle, the wizard Math, Gwydion created a wife for Llew out of the flowers of the oak, the broom, and meadowsweet. Her name was Blodeuwedd.

Llew was given land by Math and ruled it well, but his troubles were not finished. Blodeuwedd was unfaithful to him with the hunter Gronw Bebyr, and the lovers plotted to kill Llew. Blodeuwedd discovered Llew's vulnerable spot, and Gronw struck him with a poisoned spear. Screaming in agony, Llew flew away in the form of an eagle. All was not lost to the resourceful Gwydion, who recovered his son by following a sow that had been feeding on his rotting flesh, which was stuck in a tree. Gwydion turned Llew back into human form, and physicians cured his body. To punish Blodeuwedd, Gwydion turned her into an owl, and Llew himself slew Gronw.

The Legends of King Arthur

The Mabinogion contains five tales that include King Arthur: "The Lady of the Fountain," "Geraint, Son of Erbin," and "Peredur, Son of Evrawc," which are drawn from French originals, and "Culwch and Olwen" and "The Dream of Rhonabwy," which have British origins. In "Culwch and Olwen," Arthur is revealed, not as hero of chivalry, but as a fairy king, with magical powers and superhuman warriors.

We owe more to the Middle Ages and the works of Sir Thomas Malory than to the Celts for the legends of King Arthur that we know now. Arthur and the Knights of the Round Table, Lancelot and Guinevere, Sir Galahad, and Gawain and the Green Knight are thickly imbued with Christianity, although they do retain vestiges of earlier stories that are of Celtic origin, and some, like the fertility goddess Gwenhwyfar, do go back into Celtic myth . Scribes and writers in medieval times collected all sorts of stories from a variety of sources and, in trying to make coherent narratives out of them, included episodes that were never part of the original tales.

Arthur himself is believed by some to be based on the historical leader of a mobile force of cavalry in the century after the Romans left Britain, when Britain was under threat from the Saxons; his name was Ambrosius Aurelianus; but there are other versions, too. It could be that those who wove this warrior into the original Celtic legends intended to give status to what was little more than guerrilla resistance, and thus to bolster the confidence of the populace. This concept was in the tradition of Celtic storytelling: Poets and bards were meant to build up the deeds and status of their king

The Arthurian legends spread from Britain into Celtic Cornwall and Brittany. Many Arthurian heroes had close links with Brittany, where Breton storytellers were responsible for spreading their stories widely. Lancelot, Guinevere, and

Opposite: Celtic images, an ogam stone and the Green Man, from the painting Celtic Deities, *1984, by Gordon Wain. The Green Man is a mysterious figure of great natural force who has persisted in myth and folklore until modern times.*

Previous pages: Like sentinels against the sky, these standing stones at Castlenalact, in County Cork, Ireland, are carefully aligned, as if tuned meticulously to the spiritual needs of the people who set them up.

Merlin all appear in Breton legends which are mixed up with myths about the gods. Among these, the most terrible was Ankeu, the god of death and the afterlife, who, like Morrigan, marked out people before they died. Ankeu was represented as a skeleton or as a man with empty eye sockets and no nose, carrying a scythe to kill with as he rode by in his cart; those who heard its creaking axles were marked out for death.

Culwch and Olwen

Culwch did not have a good start in life. His mother went insane during her pregnancy and died shortly after his birth. His father, King Kilydd, remarried. When Culwch came of age, his stepmother told him that he must marry a maiden called Olwen or no one at all. Olwen was the daughter of Yspaddaden, the chief of the giants.

The first problem for Culwch was to find Olwen, and he sought the help of his cousin, King Arthur (though some claim that in the earliest versions of this story Arthur is not involved). He made a good impression at Arthur's court with a fine display of armor and weapons, decorated with silver and gold, so that Arthur granted his request and ordered his knights to ride with Culwch to find Olwen.

Each knight was chosen for his particular skills, and each had a magical peculiarity. The knights included Kay, who could hold his breath underwater, and go without sleep, for nine days and nights; whose sword could inflict wounds that no doctor could heal; whose subtlety was widely praised; who had the ability to stretch himself as high as the tallest tree in the forest; and the intense heat of whose nature kept all things about him warm and dry even when it rained hardest.

There was also Bedwyr (later to become Bedivere), the swiftest of all the knights, who possessed a lance that could inflict a wound nine times more terrible than any other lance, and who, despite having only one hand, could shed the blood of his enemies faster than any other knight. One of Arthur's knights went because of his extraordinary qualities as a guide; another, because he knew all the languages there were; a third, because he never returned without accomplishing the task he had been set; and a fourth, because he could cloak the other knights with invisibility.

This group of extraordinary heroes journeyed to Yspaddaden's castle, outside which they met a shepherdess who told them that Olwen came to her stream each Saturday to wash her hair. They sent a message to the castle, and Olwen duly came to the stream. Her amazing beauty immediately captured Culwch's heart, and either his arguments or his armor had the desired effect on her also, for she promised to marry him if he did whatever her father demanded. She warned her suitor that he should not give up, whatever tasks or conditions were imposed on him by her father.

Culwch and the knights went to the castle three times to ask for Olwen's hand; three times Yspaddaden told them to return the next day. And each day, as they rode away from the gates of the castle, he hurled a poisoned spear at them. The first time, one knight caught the spear and flung it back, wounding the giant's knee; the second time, another knight caught it, threw it back, and struck the giant in the breast; the third time, a third knight hurled the dart through the giant's eye, and it came out through the back of his head.

Considerably the worse for wear, Yspaddaden agreed to let Culwch have his daughter but imposed a succession of almost impossible tasks, each one involving several equally difficult subsidiary tests. Daunted at first, Culwch remembered Olwen's advice that he should agree to everything, however difficult. With the help of Arthur's knights, he accomplished all the tasks, which included the clearing,

Above: King Arthur, protected by the Virgin Mary, fighting a giant, from a sixteenth-century woodcut. Arthur relied heavily on magic to aid him as well as on his own strength and courage. Magic is often a greater element in Welsh and English Celtic lore than in Irish myth.

Opposite: Tristan playing the harp before King Mark of Cornwall, from a medieval tile in Chertsey Abbey. According to legend, Tristan was one of the knights of King Arthur's Round Table.

ploughing, and sowing of a field; the collection of materials for the wedding; and obtaining scissors from between the ears of a great boar with which to cut Yspaddaden's hair. When it looked, even then, as if Yspaddaden was going to procrastinate yet further, Culwch and his companions, finally exasperated, attacked and killed the giant. Culwch married Olwen, and they lived happily together.

Peredur and the Witches

Peredur was a warrior who first appeared in Welsh legend and resurfaces as Sir Perceval in the Arthurian legends. Like many Celtic heroes, he learned his military skills from women.

When making his way in the world, he came to a mountain castle which was under threat of attack by the nine witches of Gloucester, who had already devastated the land about. Peredur stood his ground against the first witch who attacked but agreed to let her take him to the Court of the Witches, where he stayed for three weeks, learned to be a knight, acquired a horse and weapons, and then departed.

Peredur encountered the witches again, after they had killed some of his relations and got into another fight with them. The witches realized that he was destined to kill them, for he had learned his skills from them. Peredur had to call on the help of King Arthur, and between them, they dispatched the witches of Gloucester.

Tristan and Iseult

The story of Tristan (or Tristram) and Iseult (or Isolde) was worked over frequently in medieval storytelling and in the later versions of the stories of King Arthur and the Knights of the Round Table. It was translated into many languages and portrayed in art and craft; in every way, it was a fine example of an early best-seller with enormous popularity.

In an early version of the story, which is more nearly Celtic, Tristan was the son of a prince in northwest Britain. After his parents' early death, he was brought up by a foster father in all the skills of court and warfare, in music and chess, in languages and horsemanship. But he was kidnapped by pirates and arrived eventually at the court of his uncle, King Mark of Cornwall.

In the service of King Mark, Tristan defeated the Irish giant, Morholt, who for years had been claiming an exorbitant tribute from Cornwall. Tristan himself was wounded in the fight and by chance set adrift in a small boat that carried him to Ireland, where his wounds were healed by the queen, who happened to be Morholt's sister.

To repay his debt, he slew a dragon which had been destroying the countryside and then asked for the hand of the princess Iseult on behalf of his uncle. Iseult was duly sent off with him to Cornwall, but on the way, they accidentally drank the love potion that the queen had wisely prepared for Mark and Iseult.

From that moment, Tristan and Iseult fell tragically and inextricably in love, a grand passion that took them through all manner of hardships, involved much deceit, and tore at Tristan's sense of loyalty to his uncle.

Mark finally trapped the lovers into having to admit their crime, and Tristan fled to Brittany, where he married Iseult of the White Hand, the daughter of the duke. The marriage was never consummated; it was a marriage in name only. When Tristan subsequently received a fatal wound from a poisoned arrow, he immediately called for his real love, Iseult of Ireland, with a message that, if she came to him aboard the returning ship, it should show a white sail, but if she was not aboard, it should show a black sail.

When news of the approaching ship reached Tristan, his jealous wife told him it was carrying a black sail. He died of grief, just before the safe arrival of Iseult of Ireland, who died, likewise of grief, alongside him. They were buried together, and the two trees that grew from their graves intertwined.

Chapter Five

The Celtic Way of Life

The Celts whom the Romans encountered, and who were typical of the legendary heroes, were tall and well built, with fair skin, fair hair, and blue eyes; some had flowing mustaches. Because there was no single Celtic race, there would have been considerable variations in physical appearance among those who spoke Celtic languages.

The contemporary historian Diodorus referred to short beards worn by some men and described their hair, which was smeared with lime wash and drawn back like the mane of a horse. Other evidence suggests that there were also Celts with curly or wavy hair. Cúchulainn's hair is described in the legends as multicolored and rising in stiff spikes, perhaps as a result of lime-washing the hair and dyeing it.

In the main, Celts, both men and women, would have worn a woolen garment of some kind, probably over the shoulder and tied round the waist; they might also have worn a woolen cloak, fixed with a brooch if they could afford one. The cloaks were sometimes colored in purples, crimson, or green and were sometimes multi-

Opposite: Combestone Tor, Dartmoor, England. The dramatic scenery that encompassed the Celts who lived on this high and desolate ground in the heart of Devon.

Below: A reenactment of two Celtic women spinning wool with authentic clothes and jewelry. Sheep and cattle were important to the Celts, not only for food, but also for wool and hides.

Above: Standing stones, from Castlerigg Stone Circle, near Keswick. The stones not only marked territory, but had ritual significance as well.

opposite: A page from the Book of Kells, *first created by monks in the eighth century, now kept at Trinity College, Dublin. It is one of the finest surviving early illuminated manuscripts, and a superb example of Celtic design.*

colored. Shoes, if they had them, might be made of leather. Woolen trousers were largely unknown to the Mediterranean people but were worn both tight and loose by the Celts. Trousers were typical of people from the northern, colder regions and among horse-riding people like the Thracians and Scythians

Personal decoration, such as brooches and ornaments, was important as a status symbol. Brooches of bronze might be decorated with coral or enamel and have safety-pin-type attachments. Open-ended neck rings, or torcs, with embossed ends, often in the shape of animals, were worn mainly by men. The aristocracy also wore gold bracelets and finger rings.

"Quick for Battle"

The Celts were hospitable toward strangers and recognized their social responsibilities, but the contemporary author Strabo wrote, "The whole nation is war-mad, and both high-spirited and quick for battle, although otherwise simple and not uncouth." Both men and women were renowned for their courage and their enthusiasm for fighting.

Polybius gave a good account of Celtic warriors and tactics at the Battle of

Above: In a determined effort to eliminate tribal opposition, the Romans massacred the Druids on the island of Anglesey, off the northwest corner of Wales, on the orders of the Roman governor Suetonius Paulinus.

Opposite: The Romans attempted to discredit the Celts by repeatedly criticizing the Druids' use of human ceremonial sacrifice; however, this practice may not have been as widespread as believed.

Telamon, in 225 B.C., when the Romans pushed the Gauls back from northern Italy. He referred to the naked Gaulish spearmen who fronted the battle line; these warriors had probably been brought in from outside the tribe to fight in its cause, like the free-ranging fighters, or fiana, of the Irish hero Fin mac Cumhaill. These front-line spearmen were not naked simply out of bravado; they believed that their nakedness would afford them magical protection.

Celtic tactics at the start of an encounter were to make as much noise as possible, shouting, blowing horns, and beating their shields. They worked themselves up into a frenzy in order to unsettle the opposition before the battle began, and their horsemen rode up and down in front of the enemy, throwing spears at them. Those in chariots would then dismount; there might be some preliminary challenges to individual combat; and then the main body of foot soldiers would caoe together.

Prisoners might be taken to provide slaves, but enemies were often decapitated for trophies or, more likely, as ritual sacrifices. A Roman report from Gaul in the second century B.C. noted that it was the Celts' custom to nail the heads of their enemies to the doorposts of their houses, and archaeological evidence of this practice has been found as far afield as Barcelona.

The main weapons were the sword and spear, sometimes the sling, hardly ever the bow. At various times, different types of sword were preferred. These may have had a sheath or scabbard and evolved from the shorter sword for stabbing, originally in bronze, to the longer, stronger iron sword for slashing. Daggers were used for

Right: The trees were sacred to the Celts, and the Druids practiced their religion and sought sanctuary from the Romans in the woods, which were far more plentiful than they are now.

close fighting. A warrior might carry two spears, more probably for throwing than thrusting. Wooden or leather shields had metal studs to strengthen them.

A chieftain went to battle in a light two-wheeled, two-horse war chariot with iron wheel rims, though four-wheeled wagons have also been found in tombs. Whether a warrior used horse or chariot, he would in due course alight to fight hand to hand and win personal glory. The Celts did not have stirrups, and horses were rarely used in anything like a cavalry charge, though they were an excellent vehicle for additional adornment and display. Although there were contemporary references to scythes on the wheels of chariots and to warriors' leaping onto the chariot pole between the horses, it is impossible to tell whether these were normal or exceptional practices.

Death was to be treated with respect; warriors died in expectation of a glorious afterlife. They were buried with all their trappings: with their weapons and personal ornaments, with their chariot if they had one, and with food and wine for feasting in the afterlife. Even a common grave might have a small offering of food.

Many of these characteristics of the Celtic warrior that we learn from archaeology and from Roman descriptions are corroborated by the heroics of Cúchulainn and Fin. There are sword fighting and spear throwing, champions' challenges and chariots, battle frenzy and burial rites; the common Celt, as well as the warrior, would recognize, in the tales that were told of their heroes, the reflections of their own lives.

Celtic Society

The individual Celt, within the family or tribe, did not think of himself or herself as part of a Celtic nation, though he or she might have recognized that there were other groups of people who shared certain similarities and who had some kind of loose connection. The tribe provided the social boundary for most people.

Although tribal groupings in Gaul were generally much larger than in Ireland or Britain, and there were consequent variations in how people interacted, in general customs and habits were very much the same.

The myths and legends, as well as other evidence, clearly portray the role of the elected tribal chieftain or king, who had ritual responsibilities as well as duties of leadership. Like the hero Cúchulainn and others, the chieftain was protector of his people not only against human enemies but also against the mischief of the gods and the vagaries of nature and the seasons; he must perform the proper rites to appease the gods as well as perform the necessary deeds of valor to defeat tribal foes. The role of chieftain or king was not hereditary; it required election, but successors were usually chosen from among the descendants of a common great-grandfather. The chieftain of a smaller tribe might owe allegiance to a more powerful neighbor, particularly in time of war.

In social rank, the chieftain's kinsfolk and the warrior aristocracy came next; these owed allegiance to the chieftain, probably owned land, and were patrons of

Above: Roman gladiators armed with swords often fought captive Celts, who were armed only with nets, in front of the crowds. The Romans sought to humiliate the Celts in order to bring them to submission.

109

the arts and crafts. The druids rose to this level of importance, particularly in time of war, when they directly advised the chieftain. They encompassed the roles of magicians and seers, physicians, judges, and even bards, which, accordingly, had high status in Celtic life. Next came the skilled craftspeople, and then the free commoners, the small farmers, and the minor craftspeople. In some cases, there were also those who had no rights within the community; these would have been the slaves, the vanquished, and the excommunicated.

The social structure of the gods paralleled that of the Celts themselves: Gods such as the Dagda and Lug were the chieftains, and the minor gods had particular magic or supernatural powers or particular skills and expertise in arts or crafts.

The immediate family was very important to the Celt. In law, the individual counted for very little; it was the kinship group or family that took responsibility for the actions of its members and might collectively own property. In fact, no law existed in writing until the seventh or eighth century A.D.; it existed only as the law of custom, passed on through the druids and shared by them at intertribal gatherings on festival occasions. If an individual broke this law, the kinship group was held collectively responsible.

This was an effective way to keep the peace because everyone within the group had a vested interest in keeping its members in line; in effect, there was no need for any other form of legal machinery or public administration. This arrangement also made it important for an individual to be securely linked to a kinship group, for without one, she or he had no rights and no protection.

In Wales, the oral traditions of the law were not codified until the tenth century, after which a succession of versions appeared. These included all manner of legal niceties, down to the penalty for killing the cat that guarded the king's barn, which was to pay the amount of wheat needed to cover the cat to the tip of its tail when it was held head down. There was even a set of criteria for a well-bred cat: It should have perfect ears, eyes, tail, teeth, and claws, with no marks of fire; it should kill mice and not eat its offspring; and it should not be caterwauling every new moon.

Marriage forged important links that are reflected in the myths and legends. There was marriage for common people between kinship groups and, by the aristocrats, between tribes. Marriage often involved wife purchase and the exchange of a dowry; a wealthy man might have a number of wives, one being dominant. Although the man presided over the family, women might hold high status and in some cases might own property.

Individuals coming into the tribe were immediately bound by its kinship structure. Vital links were formed between tribes not only by marriage but by the custom of putting out young aristocratic warriors to a foster parent for their education. Such alliances helped to reduce the incidence of strife between tribes, though, as the legends proved, it also caused severe problems of divided loyalties. The heroes Cúchulainn and Fin were both fostered out to learn their supernatural skills.

In their efforts to absorb the Celts, the Romans encouraged the Celtic aristocrats to adopt Roman manners and education, and they sought to undermine the personal ties of loyalty that formed the basis of Celtic society. They achieved this aim better in Gaul than in Ireland or Britain, where the Celts largely resisted the lure of Roman urban civilization.

The Druids

Much has been imagined about the druids, but little is properly known. The word druid is associated with the oak tree, the tree that was sacred to the Celts; it means "knowledge of the oak." As the priests of the Celtic people, the druids passed on most of their knowledge by word of mouth; because their knowledge was unwritten, it remained secret, and so, like many priesthoods, the druids were able to maintain their position among the people and their power over them.

There is no doubt that the druids were literate. As well as priests, they were teachers, doctors, judges, astrologers, and magicians. They were also seers, who were close to, and interpreted, the natural world for the tribe. The chieftain was the symbolic and physical leader of his tribe, but the druids represented the conti-

Above: A druid grove with an oak tree, a symbol of strength and longevity.

Left: Druid priest and priestess. Women played an important role in domestic and public life among the Celts. Some goddesses are portrayed as far more fierce than their male counterparts.

nuity of law and order and, as a result, were in many ways much more influential. Like the chieftain, they and their knowledge stood as a defense between the natural and unnatural worlds.

Through the sacred office that they held, the druids had many roles and exerted power in various ways: they were responsible for making sure that all the rituals of the tribe were performed exactly as they should be; they knew the times for sowing and harvesting; they represented a common culture between tribes; they might act as mediators in times of intertribal stress or use their skills to advise the chieftain on tactics and strategy in battle. Because they taught the aristocracy, they could influence them greatly; because they trained the bards and poets, they could control the oral traditions and the content of legends. As judges, when law and custom were broken, they were able to enforce their decisions by excommunicating the guilty person from the tribe and its vital protection.

It is likely that there were druidic "colleges," or organized groups of pupils, where oral instruction in the arts of being a druid might take as long as twenty years. Some of the early Christian monastic establishments were based on the druids's colleges. One of the central teachings of the druids, and a fundamental belief of the Celts, was that the soul survived death and passed into another body. This strong faith in immortality contributed to the success of the Celts in battle, as they had no fear of death.

The Romans recognized the powerful hold that the druids had over the Celts and did all they could to break that hold by banning the druids, destroying their sacred groves, and condemning their practices, particularly the early practice of human sacrifice. The Romans also, perhaps deliberately, confused the identity of many Celtic gods by giving them Roman names, which undermined some of the common ties of identity among the Celts. But it was the Christian church that dealt the final

Above: Reconstruction of an Iron Age Celtic village at Butser Experimental Farm in Hampshire, England. The round huts were typical of the dwellings of the ordinary people.

Opposite: Druids progressed through a long apprenticeship and steadily acquired learning and rank. Here is an arch-druid in full costume.

blow to the druids by eradicating or adapting many of their practices.

Buildings

The early Celts did not live in towns, though there were larger groupings of buildings in the areas closer to northern Italy which were more directly influenced by the Romans. The Celts were essentially a pastoral people, whose livelihood was cattle and farming, and they preferred open spaces and independence.

The Celtic family lived in a single farmstead or occasionally with a few other families in a small hamlet. It was only with the increase in trade that larger groups of houses began to provide useful market centers for the exchange of goods and information. Initially this need was served by the earth-and-stone forts that had been built mainly for military purposes.

Rectangular house plans seem to have been more popular on the European mainland, except in Spain, where round houses were also common; the round Celtic house is most commonly found in Britain and Ireland. Farmsteads sometimes had a palisade—a stone wall or bank and ditch—surrounding them as a nominal defense against attack. In some areas, such as Cornwall and Brittany, there were underground places of safety (a *souterrain*, or *fogou*), sometimes approached by a stone-lined trench. Artificial islands (crann o in Ireland) were also used for safety; they were built near the shores of lakes with a mixture of timber, brushwood, stone, clay, and peat, and with a palisade for protection.

The buildings themselves were usually made of wood, with occasional dry-stone-wall construction; they remained largely unchanged in style from prehistoric times until after the coming of the Romans. The homes of wealthier people, though equally

Right: An upright loom of the kind the Celts would have used in weaving cloth.

Below: The reconstructed interior of an Iron Age Celtic hut, with oven and pots, from Shapwick, in Somerset.

simple in construction, might have had some painted decoration or carvings.

Above: Celtic artifacts did not change much in shape from this neolithic beaker and dish from more than two thousand years before Christ.

Farming

The Celts were cattle farmers as well as crop farmers. The balance in the importance of each type of farming to each tribe depended largely on the geographical conditions in the different areas in which the Celts lived.

They first cultivated the land and laid out fields on the higher ground, on lighter, drier soil, which was less productive but easier to till. As their ploughs became heavier, and as they were able to clear the land of trees and drain the swamps, they moved down into the valleys, where the soil was richer and more productive. The Iron Age fields are often known as Celtic fields, anything up to two acres.

There is plenty of archaeological evidence of crop farming. Within farmstead sites have been found places to husk and winnow the corn, granaries for seed corn, drying racks for corn and hay, underground storage pits, iron-shod plough shares, sickles and bill hooks, and wood-working tools. The main crops were wheat and barley. The amount of corn that was exported from Britain, for example, makes it clear that there was more than enough to feed the Celtic families at home. The main animal stock were cattle, pigs, and sheep, and enclosures for them have been found as well.

Each family was largely self-sufficient. Members of the family would be skilled in a number of domestic crafts, such as cheese making, pottery making, and weaving. It was only in times of warfare that families needed to band together under strong

Right: Donkeys, or rather tame asses, need less care and food than a horse and can carry heavy loads with great patience. They have been one of the cheapest forms of transport.

Right: Donkeys, or rather tame asses, need less care and food than a horse and can carry heavy loads with great patience. They have been one of the cheapest forms of transport.

Above: Barter was the usual form of transaction for the Celts, with coins only gradually coming into use. This is a Roman coin with a double-headed Janus. The god was also known to the Celts; he faced both ways, representing gates and passageways.

leadership to defend themselves or to launch an aggressive campaign on behalf of the tribe.

Commerce

The early Celts had no use for coins, though coins were later introduced to them by the Romans. Transactions were made by barter or in the comparable value of cattle: A milk cow, for example, had a recognized value in terms of barter, and at one time, six heifers or three milk cows might buy one female slave. As trade increased outside the Celtic regions, coins became more important, and there were also metal currency bars, sometimes decorated.

Celtic communities concentrated on clothing and feeding themselves, but if they had anything left over, they could look outside the tribe to buy tools, weapons, ornaments and wine. In exchange, they could offer exports of grain, wool, animal hides, iron ore, and some tin from Cornwall and Brittany. They traded much more widely across the Mediterranean than might be imagined, and this far-reaching trade allowed the aristocrats to enhance their reputations with artifacts that were unavailable locally. As wealth increased among the Celts, the reputation of the skilled artisans also increased.

Art and Artifacts

Celtic art is often referred to as the art of La Tène culture, called after the mid-European site from which that culture stemmed. This culture spread east and west out of Gaul before Roman influence pushed it aside.

La Tène culture came from a mixture of influences. There was a native tradition

of abstract geometric design with beaten and cast metalwork, which came from trans-Alpine Europe and the cultures of Urnfield and Halstatt which preceded La Tène. Stylized birds came from eastern Mediterranean designs. Both stylized and naturalistic creatures were introduced from Asian influences, such as those of Scythia and Iran, together with the elaborate neck ornament, the torc, which was especially popular with the Celts. Creatures with strange shapes found their way from Greco-Etruscan art.

Celtic art did not simply copy these influences. Local artisans adapted ideas to produce wonderfully intricate designs based on simple motifs using gold, bronze, and sometimes silver. They created marvelous ornaments that were remarkably sophisticated, with curvilinear and asymmetrical designs in geometric and often abstract forms that craftspeople admire even today. Torcs and bracelets, brooches and rings, enabled the aristocrats to show off their wealth, and so did feasting; some of the most exquisite craft can be found in wine vessels.

Above: Cattle played an important part in Celtic life. Much of the intertribal fighting was little more than cattle raids. The Celtic myths portrayed this in the Cattle Raid of Cualnge.

Animals and Plants

In all cultures, certain animals and plants are sacred or have great significance. The Celts made marvelous use of these in their designs and motifs, and they played important parts in Celtic myths. Some animals were used in sacrifice. As the Celtic economy was based on cattle, hunting, and warfare, it is not surprising that animals such as the boar, the bull, the horse, the ram, and the stag featured prominently in Celtic life and imagery, as did birds such as the swan, the goose, the crane, and the owl.

The boar appeared in many forms throughout Europe: on the helmets of warriors, as decoration in metalwork, in stone sculpture. Boar flesh was much prized

for ritual feasts and was sometimes buried with the dead for feasts beyond the
grave. Not only the Celts but the Scandinavians believed in the supernatural boar or
pig which could be killed and eaten afresh each day. The boar was of particular significance to the Celts of Gaul and Germany and was a symbol of fertility from classical times until the Middle Ages.

The Cattle Raid of Cualnge underlines the importance of the bull in Celtic myth
and in a lifestyle where cattle raiding was probably at the heart of much tribal conflict. The significance of the bull in myth goes back three thousand years before
Christ to ancient Sumeria, where the bull god Enlil was worshiped as the god of
storm and fertility, and to the Cretan bullfights, and to the ritual place of the bull in
Greece and Rome. The Celts continued this tradition: A sacrificial bull was portrayed on the famous Gundestrup bowl, and cattle played their part in Celtic festivals.

The horse was perhaps the greatest possession a Celt could have; it also provided
the Celtic storyteller and poet with opportunities to describe the magnificent trappings of their heroes. Epona was the horse goddess of the Celts and was adopted by
the Roman cavalry as their protector. She was usually shown riding sidesaddle. Her
cult as a mother goddess spread through Spain and to eastern Europe. Horses were
frequently used as decoration on embossed artifacts. The White Horse cut into the

hillside at Uffington in Berkshire, England, survives from the Celtic Iron Age and shows the beaked head that often appeared in Celtic portrayals of the horse.

The stag was associated with the god Cernunnos, the Lord of the Animals, who wore antlers and appeared at many sites of worship, particularly in Gaul. He was a god of fertility, hunting, and regeneration; he became a god of wealth also. He usually appeared sitting cross-legged, as on the Gundestrup bowl, holding a ram-headed serpent in one hand, and with a stag next to him with similar horns. The ramheaded serpent was a symbol of power to the Celts. He survived in folklore as Herne the Hunter.

The dog was important as a hunting animal and was associated with both Cúchulainn and Fin. Cúchulainn owed his name to his fight with the great Hound of Culann, and Fin was portrayed in legend with two hounds beside him.

The goose was associated with the gods of war and remained important in later folklore. The crane had supernatural powers in Irish legends. In myth, the swan often appeared wearing chains of gold or silver that set it above other birds. It was associated with love, as in the story of Aengus and the swan maiden Caer.

Among the plants, the hazel, rowan, oak, ash, and yew were particularly important. The oak was a sacred tree throughout Europe because of its strength and longevity. Maximus of Tyre, a second-century philosopher, reported that the Celts

*Right: A stag in a wood, carved on a bench end at Bishop's
Lydeard Church in Somerset. Stag hunting was less a sport
for the Celts than a real matter of survival.*

worshiped Zeus in the form of a tall oak tree. The oak was of prime importance to
the druids. The hazel and the yew were both widely acknowledged as symbolic
trees in myth and in folklore. Throughout the world, trees have been thought of as
dwelling places for the gods, and Celtic sites of worship were invariably in groves of
trees.

The rowan was greatly valued by the druids for its protective power. As a result,
it is often found near stone circles. Even today, it is considered lucky to plant a
rowan tree near a house; to cut it down invites disaster. In the Celtic story of
Diarmaid and Grainne, when the lovers hid in the wood, Diarmaid sought permission from the guardian spirit of the trees to shelter there but then killed the spirit
in order to obtain the magic berries which had the power to restore youth to anyone who ate them. In folklore, rowanberries were said to ease childbirth.

Entertainment

Celtic life was not easy for anyone, neither for chieftain nor for commoner.
Farming and fighting were both hard. The importance of the great festivals of the
year was not simply a question of ritual appeasement; these festivals provided
much-needed relief from the struggle for survival and the anxiety that went with
everyday life.

There was horse racing at the festivals, and an early form of hurling, at which we

know that Cúchulainn excelled when he was young. He had traveled some way to reach his foster parent for his early training and came upon some youths playing "hurley." Without a word and without any help from anyone else, Cúchulainn managed to take the ball from an attacking youth and put it into the opposite goal three times in succession. The Celts also played a form of chess or checkers, and they played dice.

The best and most popular entertainment for any Celt was storytelling, with feasting and drinking at the same time. The Celts drank homemade beer or imported wine if they could afford it. At their feasts, the main dish was invariably roast pork, or pork boiled in a huge cauldron, with bread; sometimes there was beef, mutton, or fish. They sat on the ground, with hay or skins to cushion them or keep them from the cold, and listened readily to their poets and bards retelling the tales that everyone must have known by heart, but that gained richness in oratory and embroidery.

By this means, the myths and legends were kept alive without being written down, and the laws, customs, and social structures of the Celts were sustained. It seems appropriate that so much of our knowledge and understanding of these vigorous and creative people have been gained through the pleasure they took in the power of their own imagination. That is the greatest gift they have passed down to us, and we should treasure it.

Above: Silhouetted against a glowing sky, the Bocan stone circle at Inishowen, County Donegal, signifies that the physical and spiritual presence of the Celts will not be forgotten for many more thousand years.

Index

Page numbers in **boldface** indicate photo captions

Picture Credits